Over 120 recipes for

HEALTH & BEAUTY

Contents

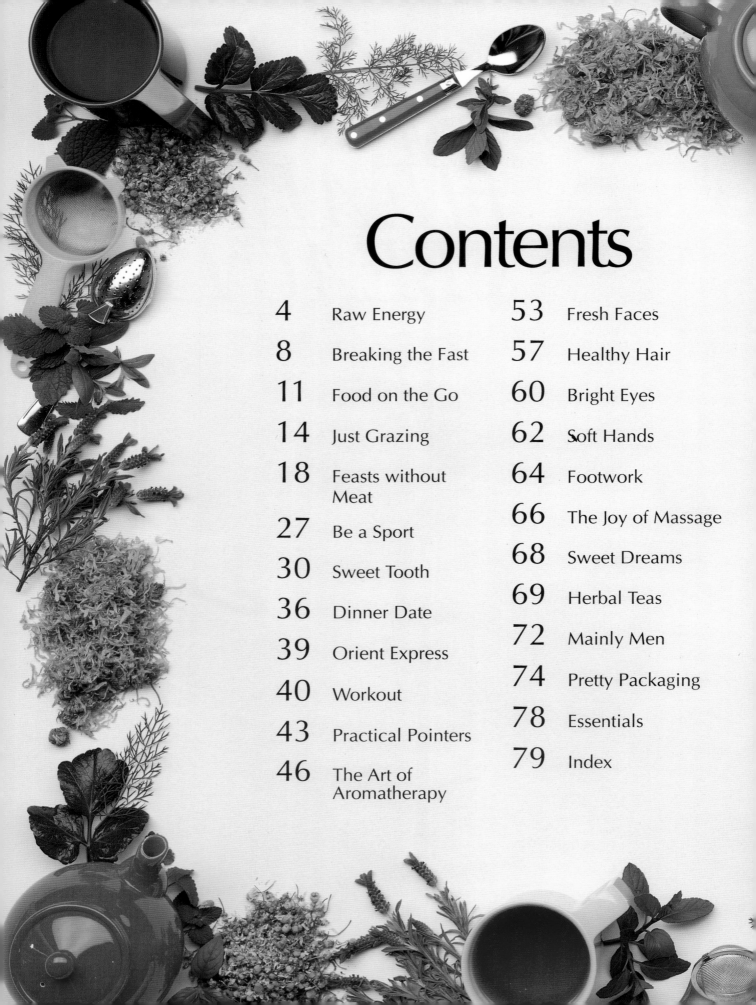

MICROWAVE IT

Where microwave instructions occur in this book a microwave oven with a 650 watt output has been used. Wattage on domestic microwave ovens varies between 500 and 700 watts, so it may be necessary to vary the cooking times slightly depending on the wattage of your oven.

CHECK-AND-GO

Use the easy Check-and-Go boxes which appear beside each ingredient. Simply check your pantry and if the ingredients are not there, tick the boxes as a reminder to add those items to your shopping list.

CANNED FOODS

Can sizes vary between countries and manufacturers. You may find the quantities in this book are slightly different to what is available. Purchase and use the can size nearest to the suggested size in the recipe.

METRIC CUPS & SPOONS

Metric	Cups	Imperial
60 mL	1/4 cup	2 fl oz
80 mL	1/3 cup	2 1/2 fl oz
125 mL	1/2 cup	4 fl oz
250 mL	1 cup	8 fl oz
	Spoons	
1.25 mL	1/4 teaspoon	
2.5 mL	1/2 teaspoon	
5 mL	1 teaspoon	
20 mL	1 tablespoon	

UK COOKERY EDITOR
Katie Swallow

UK HEALTH AND BEAUTY EDITOR
Clare Hill

TEXT
Allan Hayes

RECIPE DEVELOPMENT
Sue Geraghty, Frances Naldrett

EDITORIAL
Food Editor: Sheryle Eastwood
Assistant Food Editor: Anneka Mitchell
Home Economist: Donna Hay
Editorial Coordinator: Margaret Kelly

PHOTOGRAPHY
Andrew Payne

STYLING
Michelle Gorry

COVER DESIGN
Frank Pithers

DESIGN AND PRODUCTION
Manager: Nadia Sbisa
Senior Production Editor: Rachel Blackmore
Design and Layout: Margie Mulray
Finished Art: Chris Hatcher

PUBLISHER
Philippa Sandall

Includes Index
ISBN 1 86343 030 X

Formatted by J.B. Fairfax Press Pty Ltd
Output by Adytype, Sydney
Printed by Toppan Printing Co, Hong Kong

Family Circle is a registered trademark of IPC Magazines Ltd

Published by J. B. Fairfax Press Pty Ltd by arrangement with IPC Magazines Ltd

Distributed by J. B. Fairfax Press Ltd
9 Trinity Centre, Park Farm Estate
Wellingborough, Northants
Ph: (0933) 402330 Fax: (0933) 402234

These delicious vitality boosters will give your day a lift. What could be more natural than fresh fruit and vegetables teamed with cheese or marinated fish or simply juiced and served on ice?

Raw Energy

❖

MARINATED FISH AND AVOCADO SALAD

A delicious Mexican way of serving fish. The citrus juice 'cooks' the fish as it marinates, making it firm and white.

Serves 4

- ☐ **500 g (1 lb) firm white fish fillets such as plaice or haddock, skinned and cut into thin strips**
- ☐ **4 tablespoons lime juice**
- ☐ **4 tablespoons lemon juice**
- ☐ **2 tablespoons chopped fresh parsley**

DRESSING
- ☐ **1 clove garlic, crushed**
- ☐ **125 mL (4 fl oz) olive oil**
- ☐ **freshly ground black pepper**
- ☐ **6 drops Tabasco sauce**

SALAD
- ☐ **4 tomatoes, cut into eighths**
- ☐ **6 spring onions, trimmed and sliced lengthways**
- ☐ **1 green pepper, thinly sliced**
- ☐ **2 avocados, stoned, peeled and diced**
- ☐ **lettuce leaves**

1   Place fish in a bowl and pour over lime and lemon juices. Toss well, cover and refrigerate for 4-6 hours.
2   To make dressing, place garlic, oil, black pepper to taste and Tabasco sauce in a screwtop jar. Shake well to combine.
3   To make salad, place tomatoes, shallots, green pepper and avocados in a bowl. Pour dressing over salad and toss to combine.
4   To serve, arrange lettuce leaves on four serving plates and top with salad. Drain fish and discard marinade. Arrange fish on salad and sprinkle with parsley.

❖

ITALIAN MARINATED VEGETABLES

A crisp, tangy combination that makes an ideal starter, side dish or snack.

Serves 6

- ☐ **1 large head broccoli, cut into florets**
- ☐ **200 g (6¹/₂ oz) green beans, trimmed**
- ☐ **155 g (5 oz) baby yellow squash, sliced**
- ☐ **3 carrots, thinly sliced**
- ☐ **155 g (5 oz) mangetout, trimmed**
- ☐ **1 red pepper, thinly sliced into rings**

MARINADE
- ☐ **3 tablespoons balsamic vinegar**
- ☐ **125 mL (4 fl oz) vegetable oil**
- ☐ **1 tablespoon chopped fresh basil**
- ☐ **1 teaspoon grated lemon rind**
- ☐ **2 tablespoons honey**

1   Arrange broccoli, beans, squash, carrots, mangetout and red pepper on a large platter.
2   To make marinade, place vinegar, oil, basil, lemon rind and honey in a screwtop jar and shake to combine. Pour dressing over vegetables, cover and place in refrigerator for at least 1 hour.

Marinated Fish and Avocado Salad, Italian Marinated Vegetables, Mozzarella and Watercress Salad (page 6)

Plate and Jug Villeroy & Boch Bowl Sandy de Beyer Hat Box, Hat, Comb, Brooch and Earrings From Lois With Love

❖

MOZZARELLA AND WATERCRESS SALAD

A colourful salad of mozzarella cheese, cherry tomatoes and watercress in a fresh herb dressing.

Serves 4

- ☐ 315 g (10 oz) mozzarella, sliced
- ☐ 200 g (6½ oz) mangetout, trimmed
- ☐ 125 g (4 oz) watercress
- ☐ 250 g (8 oz) cherry tomatoes

FRESH HERB DRESSING
- ☐ 3 tablespoons olive oil
- ☐ 2 tablespoons white wine vinegar
- ☐ 2 tablespoons chopped fresh basil
- ☐ 1 tablespoon chopped fresh oregano
- ☐ freshly ground black pepper

1 To make dressing, place oil, vinegar, basil and oregano in a screwtop jar. Shake well to combine. Season to taste with black pepper. Place mozzarella in a small bowl and pour dressing over. Cover and set aside to stand for 30 minutes.

2 Boil, steam or microwave mangetout until tender. Refresh under cold water. Remove leaves from watercress. Remove mozzarella from dressing and drain, reserve dressing. Arrange mangetout, watercress, tomatoes and mozzarella on a serving platter. Pour dressing over and serve.

❖

BLOOMING SALAD WITH ROSE VINAIGRETTE

Remember when making this pretty salad that the roses need to be washed before you use them. Use a combination of different-coloured rose petals.

Serves 4

- ☐ 1 curly endive
- ☐ 1 cos lettuce
- ☐ 250 g (8 oz) yellow cherry tomatoes
- ☐ 1 cucumber, peeled and finely diced
- ☐ 15 g (½ oz) rose petals

ROSE VINAIGRETTE
- ☐ 125 mL (4 fl oz) safflower oil
- ☐ 2 teaspoons rosewater
- ☐ 1 tablespoon raspberry vinegar
- ☐ 2 teaspoons honey

1 Arrange endive, cos lettuce, tomatoes and cucumber in a large salad bowl. Gently rinse petals under cold running water and pat dry on absorbent kitchen paper. Sprinkle over salad.
2 To make vinaigrette, combine oil, rosewater, vinegar and honey in a screw-top jar and shake well to combine. Pour dressing over salad, chill and serve.

❖

STUFFED PEARS WITH BLUE DRESSING

Pears and blue cheese are natural partners, particularly in this delicious savoury dish. It is perfect as a light meal with crusty bread.

Serves 4

- ☐ 4 ripe pears, stems attached, peeled and cored
- ☐ 3 teaspoons lemon juice
- ☐ 30 g (1 oz) walnuts, finely chopped

6

- [ ] **6 fresh dates, pitted and finely chopped**
- [ ] **lettuce leaves**

BLUE CHEESE DRESSING
- [ ] **125 g (4 oz) natural yogurt**
- [ ] **1 tablespoon white wine vinegar**
- [ ] **90 g (3 oz) blue cheese, such as Stilton, Gorgonzola or Roquefort**

1 Brush pears with lemon juice. Combine walnuts and dates in a small bowl. Fill pear cavities with date mixture.

2 To make dressing, place yogurt, vinegar and cheese in a food processor or blender and process until smooth. Arrange lettuce leaves on four serving plates, top with pears and spoon dressing over. Serve immediately.

JUST JUICES

Juices are a great natural way to top up your vitamin and mineral supply.
❖ If using a blender, peel and core fruit and strain after blending.
❖ When using a juice extractor the fruit can be left whole.

Left: Blooming Salad with Rose Vinaigrette, Stuffed Pears with Blue Dressing
Below: A selection of fresh fruit juices

❖

APPLE AND CUCUMBER COOLER

A cool and refreshing juice that is a great drink for a hot summer's day.

Serves 1

- [ ] **2 apples, peeled and cored**
- [ ] **½ cucumber, peeled**

Juice apples and cucumber in a juice extractor or blender and pour over ice cubes.

❖

VITAMIN C BOOSTER

This juice supplies a real boost of vitamin C.

Serves 1

- [ ] **2 oranges, peeled**
- [ ] **2 pears, peeled and cored**
- [ ] **1 lemon, peeled**

Juice oranges, pears and lemon in a juice extractor or blender and pour over ice cubes.

❖

STRAWBERRY DELIGHT

Treat yourself to this exotic-tasting juice.

Serves 1

- [ ] **500 g (1 lb) watermelon, skin and seeds removed**
- [ ] **155 g (5 oz) strawberries, hulled**

Juice watemelon and strawberries in a juice extractor or blender and pour over ice cubes.

❖

VEGETABLE COCKTAIL

This juice is a great pick-me-up after a busy day.

Serves 1

- [ ] **2 tomatoes**
- [ ] **1 carrot**
- [ ] **2 stalks celery**
- [ ] **1 sprig fresh parsley**

Juice tomatoes, carrot, celery and parsley in a juice extractor and pour over ice.

Swizzle Sticks Sandy de Beyer *Towel Powder Blue*

Start the day right with these tasty breakfast ideas that will give you all the energy you need for an action-packed day. No need to skip breakfast anymore – we have included an easily blended cocktail for people in a hurry.

Breaking the Fast

SPICY APPLE AND BRAN MUFFINS

Makes 12
Oven temperature 180°C, 350°F, Gas 4

- [ ] **75 g (2½ oz) bran flakes**
- [ ] **250 mL (8 fl oz) milk**
- [ ] **90 g (3 oz) brown sugar**
- [ ] **4 tablespoons vegetable oil**
- [ ] **1 egg, lightly beaten**
- [ ] **90 g (3 oz) self-raising flour, sifted**
- [ ] **75 g (3½ oz) wholemeal self-raising flour, sifted and husks returned**
- [ ] **1 teaspoon ground cinnamon**
- [ ] **1 teaspoon ground nutmeg**
- [ ] **1 apple, peeled, cored and finely chopped**
- [ ] **2 teaspoons grated lemon rind**

1 Combine bran flakes and milk in a small bowl and set aside to stand for 10 minutes.

2 Place brown sugar, oil, egg and bran mixture in a bowl and mix well. Fold in self-raising and wholemeal self-raising flours, cinnamon, nutmeg, apple and lemon rind.

3 Spoon mixture into twelve lightly greased muffin tins. Bake for 20-25 minutes, or until cooked when tested with a skewer.

BAKE AHEAD MUFFINS

Muffins are a popular breakfast food. Try these delicious muffins to get your day off to a great start. You can make the muffins at the weekend and freeze them to have on hand for a quick breakfast treat. To reheat in the microwave, cook on HIGH (100%) for 30-45 seconds per muffin.

COOK'S TIP

If very large muffin tins are used, bake the muffins for 35 minutes or until cooked when tested with a skewer. These quantities will make 6 large muffins.

BLUEBERRY MUFFINS

Makes 12
Oven temperature 180°C, 350°F, Gas 4

- [ ] **155 g (5 oz) self-raising flour, sifted**
- [ ] **100 g (3½ oz) wholemeal self-raising flour, sifted and husks returned**
- [ ] **1 teaspoon ground mixed spice**
- [ ] **1 tablespoon lemon juice**
- [ ] **1 tablespoon grated lemon rind**
- [ ] **4 tablespoons muscovado sugar**
- [ ] **1 egg**
- [ ] **90 g (3 oz) butter, melted**
- [ ] **125 mL (4 fl oz) milk**
- [ ] **155 g (5 oz) blueberries, fresh, or canned and drained**

1 Place self-raising and wholemeal self-raising flours with mixed spice in a mixing bowl. Whisk together lemon juice, lemon rind, sugar, egg and butter until thick and creamy. Pour into flour mixture in bowl alternately with milk and mix until all ingredients are just combined. Gently fold in blueberries.

2 Spoon mixture into twelve greased muffin tins. Bake for 20-25 minutes, or until cooked when tested with a skewer.

❖ BANANA AND PECAN MUFFINS

Makes 12
Oven temperature 180°C, 350°F, Gas 4

- ☐ 1 egg
- ☐ 125 mL (4 fl oz) polyunsaturated oil
- ☐ 185 g (6 oz) muscovado sugar
- ☐ 125 g (4 oz) self-raising flour, sifted
- ☐ 140 g (4½ oz) wholemeal self-raising flour, sifted and husks returned
- ☐ 2 teaspoons ground mixed spice
- ☐ 1 teaspoon ground cinnamon
- ☐ 2 very ripe bananas, peeled and mashed
- ☐ 185 mL (6 fl oz) milk
- ☐ 90 g (3 oz) chopped pecan nuts
- ☐ 12 whole pecan nuts

1   Place egg, oil and sugar in a mixing bowl and mix well to combine.
2   Add self-raising and wholemeal self-raising flours, mixed spice, cinnamon, bananas, milk and chopped nuts. Spoon mixture into twelve lightly greased muffin tins. Top each muffin with a whole pecan nut. Bake for 35 minutes, or until cooked when tested with a skewer.

❖ BREAKFAST COCKTAIL

A nutritious and tasty breakfast for people in a hurry.

Serves 2

- ☐ 1 large pineapple, peeled and chopped, or 440 g (14 oz) canned pineapple chunks in unsweetened juice, drained
- ☐ 125 mL (4 fl oz) orange juice
- ☐ 60 g (2 oz) almonds
- ☐ 1 teaspoon honey
- ☐ ¼ teaspoon vanilla essence

Place pineapple, orange juice, almonds, honey and vanilla in a food processor or blender and process until smooth.

❖ HONEY TOASTED MUESLI

The amount of honey you use in this homemade muesli can be adjusted to suit your taste.

Serves 12
Oven temperature 180°C, 350°F, Gas 4

- ☐ 500 g (1 lb) rolled oats
- ☐ 100 g (3½ oz) sunflower seeds
- ☐ 3 tablespoons sesame seeds, toasted
- ☐ 45 g (1½ oz) desiccated coconut, toasted
- ☐ 100 g (3½ oz) branflakes
- ☐ 90 g (3 oz) chopped dried apricots
- ☐ 60 g (2 oz) chopped dried apples
- ☐ 90 g (3 oz) sultanas
- ☐ 4 tablespoons currants
- ☐ 250 mL (8 fl oz) honey, warmed
- ☐ 2 teaspoons ground cinnamon

1   Place oats in a thin layer on a baking tray. Bake for 10 minutes or until golden brown.
2   Combine oats, sunflower seeds, sesame seeds, coconut, branflakes, apricots, apples, sultanas and currants in a large mixing bowl.
3   Mix together honey and cinnamon and stir into muesli in bowl. Cool, then store in an airtight container.

Spicy Apple and Bran Muffins, Blueberry Muffins, Banana and Pecan Muffins, Breakfast Cocktail, Honey Toasted Muesli

Want something other than a sandwich? Try these quick and easy ideas for food on the go, or as a light meal for family and friends at the weekend.

Food on the Go

❖
CHEESE AND TOMATO SURPRISES

Fresh bread, ripe tomatoes and a taste of mango combine to make a wonderful lunch that only takes minutes to put together.

Serves 4

- ☐ **1 crusty round wholemeal loaf of bread, warmed and cut into thick slices**
- ☐ **250 g (8 oz) sliced pastrami, mortadella or garlic sausage**
- ☐ **1 lettuce, leaves separated**
- ☐ **250 g (8 oz) cherry tomatoes, halved**
- ☐ **200 g (6$\frac{1}{2}$ oz) Jarlsberg or Edam cheese, sliced**
- ☐ **60 g (2 oz) mung bean sprouts**

MANGO SPREAD
- ☐ **3 tablespoons mango chutney**
- ☐ **185 mL (6 fl oz) sour cream**
- ☐ **2 teaspoons concentrated tomato purée**
- ☐ **1 tablespoon wholegrain mustard**

1   To make spread, combine chutney, sour cream, tomato paste and mustard in a bowl.
2   Top bread with spread, then pastrami, mortadella or garlic sausage, lettuce, tomatoes, cheese and sprouts.

Cheese and Tomato Surprises, Chicken Doner Kebabs, Lattice Flans (page 12), French Toasted Sandwiches (page 12)

STAND TALL
Good posture aids digestion and will make you look taller and slimmer.
✧   The best way to stand is with your feet turned slightly outwards and about 15 cm apart. Your weight should be evenly distributed through the feet. Lift your head up as through a string is threaded through the neck and spine – this automatically lengthens your neck. Hold your chin at right angles to your neck. Allow your shoulders and arms to relax at your sides. Tipping your pelvis up and slightly forward pulls in your bottom and stomach.

❖
CHICKEN DONER KEBABS

These homemade kebabs are sure to be a winner with friends and family.

Serves 4

- ☐ **45 g (1$\frac{1}{2}$ oz) butter**
- ☐ **4 boned chicken thighs, cut into thin strips**
- ☐ **2 teaspoons curry powder**
- ☐ **$\frac{1}{2}$ teaspoon sweet chilli sauce**
- ☐ **2 tablespoons tomato sauce**
- ☐ **1 small bunch watercress**
- ☐ **1 red onion, sliced**
- ☐ **1 tomato, sliced**
- ☐ **4 large pitta breads warmed**

1   Melt butter in a small frypan and stir-fry chicken for 3 minutes or until colour changes. Stir in curry powder, chilli sauce and tomato sauce and cook for 1 minute.
2   Layer chicken, watercress, onion and tomato over pitta breads and roll up to enclose filling. Serve immediately.

❖
LATTICE FLANS

Mini crustless quiches that taste just as good warm or cold as they do hot. With a crisp green salad they make the perfect lunch for home, office or school.

Serves 4
Oven temperature 200°C, 400°F, Gas 6

- ☐ **100 g (3½ oz) spinach, stems removed, leaves chopped and cooked**
- ☐ **140 g (4½ oz) canned sweet corn kernels, drained**
- ☐ **4 eggs, lightly beaten**
- ☐ **500 mL (16 fl oz) milk**
- ☐ **125 g (4 oz) grated Edam or Gouda cheese**
- ☐ **2 tablespoons self-raising flour**
- ☐ **freshly ground black pepper**
- ☐ **2 slices lean ham, cut into strips**

1 Spread spinach and sweet corn evenly over the base of four lightly greased individual ovenproof dishes.
2 Combine eggs, milk, cheese and flour. Season to taste with black pepper and pour over spinach and corn in dishes. Arrange ham strips on top of egg mixture in lattice pattern and bake for 15-20 minutes or until firm.

❖
FRENCH TOASTED SANDWICHES

In France these tasty sandwiches known as 'Croque Monsieur' are sold in cafés. Any of your favourite fillings can be used in them.

Serves 4

- ☐ **8 slices brown bread, crusts removed**
- ☐ **4 slices lean ham, finely chopped**
- ☐ **315 g (10 oz) canned asparagus tips, drained and mashed**
- ☐ **125 g (4 oz) grated Emmenthal or Gruyère cheese**
- ☐ **3 eggs, well beaten**
- ☐ **5 tablespoons milk**

1 Roll bread slices out flat using a rolling pin. Layer half of each slice, diagonally with ham, asparagus and cheese. Fold uncovered half over filling and press flat. Secure with toothpicks to enclose filling.
2 Combine egg and milk in a shallow dish. Dip each filled bread triangle in egg mixture. Heat a nonstick frypan and cook sandwiches until golden brown on both sides. Serve immediately.

❖
RICE CAKE PIZZAS

Rice cakes are puffed rice formed into a pattie shape. They make a light, healthy and nutritious alternative to bread. You could use pitta bread, crumpets or wholegrain bread instead.

Serves 4

- ☐ **8 rice cakes**
- ☐ **1 large tomato, sliced**
- ☐ **8 slices salami or pastrami**
- ☐ **8 mushrooms, sliced**
- ☐ **1 small red pepper, sliced**
- ☐ **125 g (4 oz) grated mozzarella cheese**
- ☐ **2 tablespoons chopped fresh basil leaves**

Top each rice cake with slices of tomato, salami or pastrami, mushrooms and red pepper, and sprinkle with cheese and basil. Place under a grill preheated to medium high and cook for 3 minutes, or until cheese melts.

HEALTH TIP

To enhance the absorption of iron from breads, cereals and vegetables, eat them with foods rich in vitamin C, such as citrus fruits and juices. Avoid consuming tea and coffee at the same time, as the tannins, particularly in tea, reduce the absorption of the iron.

Corn and Carrot Filo Parcels, Rice Cake Pizzas, Apricot Chicken Burgers

Platter, Bottle and Cups Made in Japan Towel Powder Blue

❖

CORN AND CARROT FILO PARCELS

Corn and carrots wrapped in filo pastry make a delicious light meal that can be eaten hot, warm or cold. A mixed lettuce and fresh herb salad and wholemeal rolls are the perfect accompaniments if you want something a little more substantial.

Serves 4
Oven temperature 180°C, 350°F, Gas 4

- [ ] **45 g (1¹/₂ oz) butter**
- [ ] **1 red onion, chopped**
- [ ] **200 g (6¹/₂ oz) ricotta cheese**
- [ ] **1 egg, lightly beaten**
- [ ] **4 carrots, grated**
- [ ] **60 g (2 oz) slivered almonds, toasted**
- [ ] **2 tablespoons sweet corn relish**
- [ ] **140 g (4¹/₂ oz) canned sweet corn kernels, drained**
- [ ] **60 g (2 oz) grated cheddar cheese**
- [ ] **freshly ground black pepper to taste**
- [ ] **8 sheets filo pastry**
- [ ] **1 tablespoon poppy seeds**

1   Melt half the butter in a frypan. Cook onion for 3 minutes or until soft. Remove from pan and combine with ricotta cheese, egg, carrots, almonds, relish, sweet corn, cheese and black pepper in a bowl.
2   Melt remaining butter. Layer four sheets filo pastry, brushing between each layer with butter. Repeat with remaining pastry and butter. Cut each layered pile in half crossways.
3   Place a quarter of carrot mixture along short side, roll up pastry around filling, envelope style. Brush with any remaining butter and sprinkle with poppy seeds. Transfer rolls to a lightly greased baking oven tray and bake for 30 minutes, or until golden brown.

❖

APRICOT CHICKEN BURGERS

Serves 4

- [ ] **1¹/₂ tablespoons natural low-fat yogurt or mayonnaise**
- [ ] **2 tablespoons snipped fresh chives**
- [ ] **4 plain or wholemeal hamburger buns, rolls or pitta breads**
- [ ] **1 small ripe avocado, stoned, peeled and sliced**
- [ ] **1 gem lettuce, leaves shredded**

CHICKEN BURGERS
- [ ] **250 g (8 oz) lean minced chicken**
- [ ] **1 egg, lightly beaten**
- [ ] **5 dried apricots, finely chopped**
- [ ] **1 small carrot, grated**
- [ ] **1 small courgette, grated**
- [ ] **30 g (1 oz) grated Edam or Gouda cheese**

1   Combine yogurt or mayonnaise and chives. Split buns, rolls or pitta breads and spread with yogurt or mayonnaise mixture. Set aside.
2   To make burgers, combine minced chicken, egg, apricots, carrot, courgette and cheese in a bowl. Divide mixture into four equal portions and shape each portion into a pattie. Cook patties in a nonstick frying pan for 6-7 minutes on each side, or until golden brown and cooked.
3   To assemble burgers, place cooked patties inside prepared buns and top with avocado and lettuce.

Some people like to eat little and often –
to graze. This selection of sweet and savoury snacks
offers something for everyone, be it tasty, nutritious, a
source of instant energy, or a simple indulgence
like Mango and Almond Dip.

Just Grazing

❖

SALMON SCROLLS

*Smoked salmon with a tasty filling
makes a perfect treat. Or you might like
to serve these scrolls with a mixed
lettuce and fresh herb salad as
a starter or light meal.*

Serves 2

- ☐ **4 slices smoked salmon**
- ☐ **1 tablespoon chopped fresh parsley**
- ☐ **2 teaspoons chopped fresh dill**

FILLING
- ☐ **125 g (4 oz) cream cheese**
- ☐ **2 tablespoons sour cream**
- ☐ **2 teaspoons wholegrain mustard**
- ☐ **2 teaspoons lemon juice**
- ☐ **freshly ground black pepper**

1   Place salmon in a rectangle shape on a piece of plastic food wrap.
2   To make filling, beat together cream cheese, sour cream, mustard, lemon juice and black pepper to taste. Spread evenly over salmon slices and sprinkle with parsley and dill.
3   Roll up salmon widthways, like a Swiss roll, cover and refrigerate until firm. To serve, cut into 1 cm (½ in) rounds.

❖

AUBERGINE DIP WITH FRESH VEGETABLES

Serves 4
Oven temperature 200°C, 400°F, Gas 6

- ☐ **1 large aubergine**
- ☐ **4 tablespoons natural yogurt**
- ☐ **2 tablespoons lemon juice**
- ☐ **3 tablespoons chopped fresh parsley**
- ☐ **2 cloves garlic, crushed**
- ☐ **2 tablespoons olive oil**
- ☐ **1 tablespoon tahini paste**

- ☐ **fresh parsley sprigs**
- ☐ **paprika**
- ☐ **a selection of mangetout, carrot sticks, cauliflower florets and radishes to serve**

1   Prick aubergine in several places with a fork and place in an ovenproof dish. Bake for 40-45 minutes or until tender. Set aside until cool enough to handle.
2   Peel skin off aubergine and roughly chop flesh. Place aubergine flesh, yogurt, lemon juice, parsley, garlic, oil and tahini paste in a food processor or blender and process until smooth. Transfer to a bowl and garnish with parsley sprigs and paprika. Serve with vegetables.

❖

FRUITY APRICOT COOKIES

*These tasty cookies, full of
dried fruit, look and taste terrific.
Great as an after-school
or work snack.*

Makes 25
Oven temperature 180°C, 350°F, Gas 4

- ☐ **125 g (4 oz) butter**
- ☐ **125 g (4 oz) brown sugar**
- ☐ **½ teaspoon ground cinnamon**
- ☐ **1 egg**
- ☐ **60 g (2 oz) self-raising flour**
- ☐ **75 g (2½ oz) wholemeal self-raising flour**
- ☐ **20 g (¾ oz) wheat germ**
- ☐ **4 tablespoons desiccated coconut**
- ☐ **45 g (1½ oz) rolled oats**
- ☐ **80 g (2½ oz) dried apricots, chopped**
- ☐ **60 g (2 oz) dried apples, chopped**
- ☐ **3 tablespoons currants**

1   Place butter and sugar in a bowl and beat until light and fluffy. Stir in egg, then fold in self-raising and wholemeal flours, wheat germ, coconut, rolled oats, apricots, apples and currants. Mix to combine.

2   Roll spoonfuls of mixture into balls, place on lightly greased oven trays and flatten slightly with a fork. Bake for 10-12 minutes, or until biscuits are firm. Remove from oven and cool on tray.

❖

RICE CAKES WITH THREE TOPPINGS

*Rice cakes are a great base for quick
snacks. They are a light and nutritious
alternative to bread.*

Each topping is enough for 4 rice cakes

- ☐ **4 rice cakes**

FRUITY TOPPING
- ☐ **3 tablespoons low-calorie strawberry jam**
- ☐ **2 bananas, peeled and sliced**
- ☐ **2 tablespoons sunflower seeds**

Spread rice cakes with jam, top with banana slices and sprinkle with sunflower seeds.

NUTTY CHEESE TOPPING
- ☐ **2 tablespoons peanut butter**
- ☐ **125 g (4 oz) cottage cheese**
- ☐ **1 apple, cored and sliced**

Spread rice cakes with peanut butter, top with cottage cheese and apple slices.

SALMON TOPPING
- ☐ **220 g (7 oz) canned salmon, drained**
- ☐ **3 tablespoons natural yogurt or sour cream**
- ☐ **2 teaspoons lemon juice**
- ☐ **2 teaspoons French mustard**
- ☐ **freshly ground black pepper to taste**
- ☐ **30 g (1 oz) beansprouts**

Mix together salmon, yogurt or sour cream, lemon juice, mustard and black pepper. Place beansprouts on rice cakes and top with salmon mixture.

*Rice Cakes with Three Toppings,
Salmon Scrolls, Aubergine Dip with Fresh
Vegetables, Fruity Apricot Cookies,
Energy Bars (page 16)*

6 ESSENTIAL WATER FACTS

1 Water is the second most important element required for living. The most important is, of course, air.

2 The adult body is 60-70 per cent water. Water is vital for the chemical reactions that occur in the body. It carries nutrients and oxygen to the cells, lubricates the joints and helps keep the body cool through perspiration.

3 You should drink eight to ten glasses of water a day. This may seem a lot but you should remember that you lose at least two to three litres of water from your body a day and this must be replaced. Of course the more active you are the more water you lose and therefore the more you need to replace.

4 Water can be replaced by eating fruit and vegetables with a high water content, by drinking milk, fruit juices, soup and soft drinks. However, the best way to replace water is to drink it. Plain water is most efficiently absorbed by the body.

5 Caffeinated drinks such as coffee are not good replacement fluids, as caffeine causes you to lose even more fluid. Alcohol has the same effect.

6 Feeling thirsty is your body's way of telling you that you are running low on fluids.

❖

ENERGY BARS

Great to have tucked into your bag for a quick boost of energy during the day.

Makes 20

- ☐ 60 g (2 oz) puffed rice cereal
- ☐ 75 g (2¹/₂ oz) bran flakes, lightly crushed
- ☐ 75 g (2¹/₂ oz) shredded coconut
- ☐ 60 g (2 oz) dried apricots, chopped
- ☐ 30 g (1 oz) dried apples, chopped
- ☐ 60 g (2 oz) glacé pineapple, chopped
- ☐ 90 g (3 oz) sultanas
- ☐ 1 teaspoon ground cinnamon

- ☐ 90 g (3 oz) brown sugar
- ☐ 90 g (3 oz) butter
- ☐ 125 mL (4 fl oz) honey
- ☐ 125 mL (4 fl oz) coconut cream

1 Combine rice cereal, bran flakes, coconut, apricots, apples, pineapple, sultanas and cinnamon in a large mixing bowl.
2 Place brown sugar, butter, honey and coconut cream in a small saucepan. Stir over low heat until mixture combines. Bring to the boil, lower heat and simmer for 5 minutes, or until mixture is thick and syrupy. Pour over dry ingredients and mix well. Press into a greased and lined 15 x 25 cm (6 x 10 in) shallow cake tin and refrigerate until set. Cut into fingers.

❖

MANGO AND ALMOND DIP

Makes 500 g (1 lb)

- ☐ 1 mango, peeled and stoned
- ☐ 2 tablespoons icing sugar, sifted
- ☐ 3 tablespoons flaked almonds, toasted
- ☐ 315 mL (10 fl oz) double cream, whipped

Place mango and icing sugar in a food processor or blender and process until smooth. Place in a bowl and fold in almonds and cream. Chill and serve with fresh fruit.

❖

PINA COLADA DIP

Makes 500 g (1 lb)

- ☐ 250 g (8 oz) cream cheese
- ☐ 440 g (14 oz) canned crushed pineapple, drained
- ☐ 3 tablespoons shredded coconut, toasted
- ☐ 3 tablespoons cream
- ☐ 1 tablespoon Malibu (optional)

Beat cream cheese until smooth. Stir in pineapple, coconut, cream and Malibu. Chill and serve with fresh fruit.

❖

CROSTINI

A super quick snack made from store cupboard ingredients. Top with olives and red pepper just before serving if you wish.

Serves 2

- ☐ 1 clove garlic, crushed
- ☐ 8 black olives, pitted and finely chopped

- ☐ 1 tablespoon capers, finely chopped
- ☐ 4 tablespoons olive oil
- ☐ 4 slices wholemeal bread, crusts removed and slices cut in half
- ☐ 90 g (3 oz) mozzarella cheese, thinly sliced

1 Place garlic, olives, capers and 1 tablespoon oil in a food processor or blender and process until smooth. Spread garlic mixture over half the bread slices. Top with cheese and remaining bread slices.
2 Brush top of each sandwich with oil and cook under a preheated grill until lightly browned. Turn over and brush with remaining oil and grill until brown.

❖

PITTA CRISPS

Serves 4
Oven temperature 180°C, 350°F, Gas 4

- ☐ 6 round pitta breads
- ☐ 4 tablespoons oil

CHEESY TOPPING
- ☐ 60 g (2 oz) grated Parmesan cheese
- ☐ 2 teaspoons paprika
- ☐ ¹/₂ teaspoon chilli powder

1 Split each pitta bread into two. Brush lightly with oil.
2 To make topping, mix together Parmesan cheese, paprika and chilli powder. Sprinkle over bread. Place pitta breads on oven tray and bake for 10 minutes, or until crisp. Allow to cool and break into small crisps.

Mango and Almond Dip, Pina Colada Dip, Pitta Crisps, Crostini

17

Whether served as starters or mains, these meals without meat will have family and friends coming back for seconds.

Feasts without Meat

❖

CHUNKY HOTPOT

Serves 4

- ☐ 2 tablespoons vegetable oil
- ☐ 1 clove garlic, crushed
- ☐ 1 small fresh red chilli, chopped
- ☐ 1 onion, chopped
- ☐ 2 teaspoons curry powder
- ☐ 2 teaspoons ground cumin
- ☐ 1 teaspoon garam masala
- ☐ 2 tablespoons chopped fresh coriander
- ☐ 1 tablespoon chopped fresh ginger
- ☐ 1 head broccoli, broken into small florets
- ☐ 3 carrots, chopped
- ☐ 2 parsnips, chopped
- ☐ 1 large potato, cubed
- ☐ 375 g (12 oz) baby squash, halved
- ☐ 1 tablespoon plain flour
- ☐ 375 mL (12 fl oz) water
- ☐ 200 mL (6^1/$_2$ fl oz) coconut cream
- ☐ 125 g (4 oz) roasted cashew nuts, chopped

1   Heat oil in a large saucepan, cook garlic, chilli, onion, curry powder, cumin, garam masala, coriander and ginger over a low heat for 1 minute. Add broccoli, carrots, parsnips, potato and squash. Cook for 5-8 minutes over a medium heat.
2   Stir in flour and cook for 1 minute. Remove pan from heat and gradually blend in water. Cook over a medium heat, stirring constantly until mixture boils and thickens. Reduce heat, cover and simmer for 10-15 minutes, or until vegetables are tender.
3   Whisk in coconut cream and cook over a low heat for 2-3 minutes. Spoon into individual bowls and sprinkle with cashew nuts to serve.

❖

POTATO AND PESTO BAKE

Serves 4
Oven temperature 180°C, 350°F, Gas 4

- ☐ 8 potatoes, washed and thickly sliced

PESTO
- ☐ 60 g (2 oz) fresh basil leaves
- ☐ 2 cloves garlic, crushed
- ☐ 2 tablespoons pine nuts
- ☐ 125 mL (4 fl oz) olive oil
- ☐ 4 tablespoons grated fresh Parmesan cheese

TOPPING
- ☐ 315 mL (10 fl oz) light sour cream
- ☐ 60 g (2 oz) grated cheddar cheese
- ☐ freshly ground black pepper

1   Boil, steam or microwave potato slices until almost tender. Drain and layer potatoes in the bottom of a greased ovenproof dish.
2   To make Pesto, place basil, garlic, pine nuts, oil and Parmesan in food processor or blender and process until smooth. Spread over potatoes.
3   To make topping, spoon sour cream over pesto and top with cheese and black pepper to taste. Bake for 10 minutes or until potatoes are soft and top is golden brown.

Chunky Hotpot, Potato and Pesto Bake, Singapore Noodle Stir-Fry (page 20)

SINGAPORE NOODLE STIR-FRY

Serves 4

- ☐ 375 g (12 oz) rice noodles
- ☐ 1 tablespoon sesame oil
- ☐ 1 onion, chopped
- ☐ 1 tablespoon sesame seeds
- ☐ 2 red chillies, chopped
- ☐ 185 g (6 oz) sliced bamboo shoots
- ☐ 4 tablespoons bean sprouts
- ☐ ¼ cabbage, finely shredded
- ☐ 1 carrot, finely chopped
- ☐ 1 red pepper, diced

SAUCE
- ☐ 3 tablespoons plum sauce
- ☐ 1 tablespoon sugar
- ☐ 1 tablespoon white wine vinegar
- ☐ 185 mL (6 fl oz) vegetable stock
- ☐ 2 teaspoons cornflour blended with 1 tablespoon of water

1   Place noodles in a large saucepan of boiling water and cook until tender. Drain and set aside.

2   Heat oil in pan, add onion and cook 3 minutes or until tender. Stir in sesame seeds and chillies, and cook for 2 minutes.

3   Add bamboo shoots, bean sprouts, cabbage, carrot and red pepper. Cook for 5 minutes, stirring frequently.

4   To make sauce, combine plum sauce, sugar, vinegar and stock. Add to pan with vegetables. Bring to the boil, then reduce heat and simmer for 2 minutes. Pour in cornflour mixture, and stir until mixture thickens slightly. Toss through noodles and serve immediately.

Indonesian Cooked Salad

Platter Hale Imports Carpet Mosman Carpets Address Book and Pens Made In Japan

FIBRE FACTS

Fibre is nature's appetite suppressant and bulking agent. It creates a feeling of fullness and may put a brake on overeating.

✧   Soluble fibre, found in oats, dried peas, beans, rice, barley and certain fruits, has the ability to remove cholesterol from the body.

INDONESIAN COOKED SALAD

Pappadams are the perfect accompaniment to this unusual salad of lightly cooked vegetables topped with eggs and a spicy peanut sauce.

Serves 4

- ☐ 2 potatoes, cut into chunks
- ☐ 4 carrots, sliced
- ☐ 250 g (8 oz) green beans, sliced
- ☐ 250 g (8 oz) spinach, stalks removed
- ☐ 2 tablespoons vegetable oil
- ☐ 125 g (4 oz) bean sprouts
- ☐ 1 small cucumber, cut into sticks
- ☐ 1 large onion, sliced
- ☐ 2 hard-boiled eggs, quartered

PEANUT SAUCE
- ☐ 1 tablespoon vegetable oil
- ☐ 1 small onion, chopped
- ☐ 1 clove garlic, crushed
- ☐ 250 mL (8 fl oz) coconut milk
- ☐ 1 tablespoon lemon juice
- ☐ 5 tablespoons peanut butter
- ☐ ½ teaspoon chilli powder
- ☐ 1 bay leaf

1   Boil, steam or microwave potatoes, carrots, beans and spinach, separately, until just tender. Drain and layer in a deep dish.

2   Heat 1 tablespoon oil in a wok or frying pan and stir-fry bean sprouts and cucumber for 2-3 minutes. Drain and sprinkle over vegetables in dish. Heat remaining oil in pan and cook onion for 4-5 minutes or until golden. Drain and set aside.

3   To make sauce, heat oil in a saucepan and cook onion and garlic for 4-5 minutes, or until onion softens. Stir in coconut milk, lemon juice, peanut butter, chilli powder and bay leaf. Cook over a medium heat, stirring constantly, until mixture thickens.

3   Arrange egg over vegetables, pour sauce over and top with onions.

Baking Dish and Bowl/ Hale Imports

Vegetable Pasta Bake

❖

VEGETABLE PASTA BAKE

A lighter version of lasagne. This delicious dish uses instant lasagne without the heavy traditional sauce.

Serves 6
Oven temperature 180°C, 350°F, Gas 4

- ☐ **9 wholemeal no pre-cooking required lasagne sheets**
- ☐ **250 g (8 oz) silken tofu, beaten until smooth**

FILLING
- ☐ **1 tablespoon olive oil**
- ☐ **¼ cabbage, shredded**
- ☐ **1 carrot, finely chopped**
- ☐ **1 large green pepper, de-seeded and finely chopped**
- ☐ **1 large red pepper, de-seeded and finely chopped**
- ☐ **315 g (10 oz) canned sweet corn kernels, drained**
- ☐ **440 g (14 oz) canned peeled tomatoes, undrained and mashed**
- ☐ **5 tablespoons chopped fresh basil**
- ☐ **freshly ground black pepper**

TOPPING
- ☐ **125 g (4 oz) grated mozzarella cheese**
- ☐ **30 g (1 oz) wholemeal breadcrumbs, made from stale bread**
- ☐ **4 tablespoons chopped walnuts**

1 To make filling, heat oil in a saucepan, cook cabbage, carrot, green and red peppers, sweet corn, tomatoes and basil over a medium heat until boiling. Reduce heat and simmer for 15 minutes or until vegetables are soft and mixture reduces and thickens. Season to taste with black pepper.

2 To make topping, combine cheese, breadcrumbs and walnuts in a bowl and set aside.

3 Spread one-third of filling over base of lightly greased 20 x 30 cm (8 x 12 in) ovenproof dish. Cover with a layer of lasagne sheets, spread with 75 g (2½ oz) tofu, then one-third of filling mixture. Repeat layers, finishing with lasagne. Spread with remaining tofu and sprinkle with topping. Bake for 30-35 minutes or until tender.

DON'T SKIP MEALS

Skipping meals often leads to consuming more kilojoules (calories), not less. When you feel deprived, there's always the temptation to make up for it with a snack. Skipping breakfast makes a morning snack hard to resist.

✧ Missing meals also slows down your metabolism and makes it harder for your body to burn fat.

4 EASY STEPS TO LESS SALT

Once you reduce the amount of salt you eat you'll notice how salty many foods taste and the thirst they create.

1   Stop sprinkling salt on food. It will take your tastebuds three to four weeks to adjust to a lower salt level.

2   Stop cooking with salt. Many of the foods that you cook with actually contain salt and additional salt is not necessary. Try using fresh herbs as a flavour booster.

3   Start buying salt-reduced or salt-free bread, rolls, crispbread, butter and polyunsaturated margarine. This will drop your salt intake significantly, particularly if you eat a lot of bread.

4   Start shopping for low-salt, salt-reduced or no-added-salt varieties of your regular groceries. More and more products are available in a light or salt-reduced form.

❖

AVOCADO SALAD WITH SPICY DRESSING

Serves 4

☐ **2 avocados, stoned, peeled, and sliced**
☐ **2 small tomatoes, cut into wedges**
☐ **125 g (4 oz) olives, pitted**
☐ **1 lettuce, separated into leaves**

SPICY DRESSING
☐ **4 tablespoons olive oil**
☐ **3 tablespoons lemon juice**
☐ **2 tablespoons concentrated tomato purée**
☐ **1 teaspoon chilli powder**
☐ **¹/₂ teaspoon ground cumin**
☐ **freshly ground black pepper**

1   To make dressing, place oil, lemon juice, tomato paste, chilli powder, cumin, and black pepper to taste in a food processor or blender and process until smooth.
2   Place avocados, tomatoes and olives in a bowl, pour dressing over and toss to combine. Cover and place in the refrigerator to marinate for 30 minutes.
3   Arrange lettuce leaves on a serving platter and top with salad.

Avocado Salad with Spicy Dressing, Colourful Potato Salad

❖

COLOURFUL POTATO SALAD

Serves 6

☐ **750 g (1¹/₂ lb) potatoes, washed**
☐ **vegetable oil**
☐ **2 stalks celery, finely chopped**
☐ **1 large cucumber, diced**
☐ **2 green peppers, diced**
☐ **2 carrots, grated**
☐ **1 raw beetroot, peeled and grated**
☐ **1 small lettuce, leaves torn into bite-size pieces**
☐ **30 g (1 oz) alfalfa sprouts**
☐ **3 tablespoons mayonnaise**
☐ **2 avocados, stoned, peeled, and sliced**

1   Boil, steam or microwave potatoes until tender. While still hot, cut into large pieces and place in a bowl. Sprinkle with oil.
2   Add celery, cucumber, green peppers, carrots, beetroot, lettuce, sprouts and mayonnaise to bowl and toss to combine. Top with avocado slices and serve.

❖

CHAMPAGNE TEMPURA

Serves 4

- ☐ 8 small cauliflower florets
- ☐ 8 button mushrooms
- ☐ 12 green beans, trimmed
- ☐ 1 red pepper, sliced into rings
- ☐ 1 green apple, cored and sliced
- ☐ 2 slices pineapple, quartered
- ☐ oil for deep-frying

BATTER
- ☐ 90 g (3 oz) self-raising flour, sifted
- ☐ 60 g (2 oz) cornflour, sifted
- ☐ 1 egg, lightly beaten
- ☐ 125 mL (4 fl oz) iced water
- ☐ 125 mL (4 fl oz) chilled champagne
- ☐ 2 ice cubes

DIPPING SAUCE
- ☐ 3 tablespoons sour cream
- ☐ 3 tablespoons mayonnaise
- ☐ 1 tablespoon chopped fresh herbs

1 To make batter, place flour and cornflour in a bowl. Mix together egg, water and champagne. Pour into flour mixture and stir until smooth. Do not over-beat. Place ice cubes in batter.

2 Heat oil in a large saucepan. Dip cauliflower, mushrooms, beans, red pepper, apple and pineapple pieces into batter and cook a few pieces at a time in oil until golden brown. Remove from oil and drain on absorbent kitchen paper.

3 To make sauce, mix together sour cream, mayonnaise and herbs. Serve as a dipping sauce with hot vegetables.

❖

ROASTED PEPPER FRITTATA

Serve with crusty bread and a salad.

Serves 4

- ☐ 1 red pepper, halved and seeded
- ☐ 1 green pepper, halved and seeded
- ☐ 2 tablespoons oil
- ☐ 1 leek, finely chopped
- ☐ 6 eggs
- ☐ 170 mL (5½ fl oz) milk
- ☐ 2 tablespoons snipped fresh chives
- ☐ 4 tablespoons grated Cheddar cheese
- ☐ freshly ground black pepper
- ☐ 2 tablespoons grated Parmesan cheese

1 Place red and green peppers under a hot grill. Cook until skin is charred. Remove peppers from grill, place in plastic bag, seal and allow to stand for 10 minutes.

2 Remove peppers from plastic bag and peel away skins. Slice thinly and set aside.

3 Heat oil in a frypan, and cook leek for 2 minutes or until tender. Whisk together eggs, milk, chives, cheese and black pepper. Place peppers in pan, pour egg mixture over and sprinkle with Parmesan cheese. Cook over a low heat until frittata is set. Place under a preheated grill for 3-4 minutes or until golden brown.

Champagne Tempura, Roasted Pepper Frittata

Sauce Dish Hale Imports *Tissue Cover* From Lois With Love

❖

BEANY GOLDEN PUMPKINS

Serves 4
Oven temperature 180°C, 350°F, Gas 4

- ☐ **4 small golden pumpkins**
- ☐ **1 tablespoon vegetable oil**

FILLING

- ☐ **1 tablespoon vegetable oil**
- ☐ **1 onion, chopped**
- ☐ **1 small red chilli, finely chopped**
- ☐ **3 teaspoons ground cumin**
- ☐ **1 clove garlic, crushed**
- ☐ **1 stalk celery, chopped**
- ☐ **125 g (4 oz) button mushrooms, chopped**
- ☐ **2 tablespoons concentrated tomato purée**
- ☐ **440 g (14 oz) canned, chopped, and peeled tomatoes**
- ☐ **315 g (10 oz) canned kidney beans, rinsed**

1   Cut a slice from top of pumpkins, remove seeds. Brush inside and outside shells and tops with oil. Replace tops on pumpkins and arrange on a baking tray. Bake for 30 minutes or until tender.

2   To make filling, heat oil in a saucepan. Cook onion, chilli, cumin and garlic over a medium heat for 3 minutes. Stir in celery, mushrooms, tomato purée and tomatoes. Bring to the boil, then reduce heat and simmer for 15 minutes, or until mixture reduces and thickens.

3   Add beans and cook over a medium heat for 2-3 minutes. Spoon mixture into pumpkin shells to serve.

❖

CAULIFLOWER CROQUETTES

Serves 4
Oven temperature 180°C, 350°F, Gas 4

- ☐ **1 cauliflower, broken into florets**
- ☐ **2 eggs, lightly beaten**
- ☐ **30 g (1 oz) unprocessed bran**
- ☐ **4 tablespoons ricotta cheese**
- ☐ **2 tablespoons chopped fresh parsley**
- ☐ **3 tablespoons snipped fresh chives**
- ☐ **60 g (2 oz) grated Cheddar cheese**

1   Boil, steam or microwave cauliflower until very tender, then mash well.

2   Add eggs, bran, ricotta cheese, parsley and chives. Mix well and shape into croquettes. Place in a lightly greased ovenproof dish, sprinkle with cheese and bake for 20 minutes.

CARROT TIMBALES WITH HERB SAUCE

A colourful and interesting dish which can be prepared in advance and baked when required.

Serves 6
Oven temperature 200°C, 400°F, Gas 6

- ☐ **6 carrots, sliced**
- ☐ **30 g (1 oz) butter**
- ☐ **2 egg yolks**
- ☐ **freshly ground black pepper**
- ☐ **125 g (4 oz) large spinach leaves**

FRESH HERB SAUCE
- ☐ **15 g (¹/₂ oz) butter**
- ☐ **2 tablespoons plain flour**
- ☐ **250 mL (8 fl oz) milk**
- ☐ **1 tablespoon chopped fresh parsley**
- ☐ **1 tablespoon snipped fresh chives**
- ☐ **1 tablespoon chopped fresh mint**
- ☐ **freshly ground black pepper**

1 Boil, steam or microwave carrots until tender. Set aside and allow to cool. Place carrots, butter and egg yolks in a food processor or blender and process until smooth. Season to taste with black pepper.

2 Lightly grease six individual timbale moulds or ramekins. Blanch spinach leaves and use to line moulds, allowing some of the leaves to overhang the top. Spoon carrot mixture into moulds and fold over spinach leaves to cover. Cook for 25-30 minutes or until set.

3 To make sauce, melt butter in a saucepan, stir in flour and cook for 1 minute, stirring frequently. Gradually stir in milk and cook over a medium heat, stirring constantly, until sauce boils and thickens. Add parsley, chives and mint and season to taste with black pepper. Serve hot sauce with timbales.

Left: Beany Golden Pumpkins, Cauliflower Croquettes
Below: Carrot Timbales with Herb Sauce

Tiles Pazotti Platter, Sauceboat, Ladle and Covered Dish Villeroy & Boch Headband From Lois With Love

Active lifestyles need energy. Make sure that
the right food is part of your daily workout and
you'll have a recipe for success.

Be a Sport

❖

SMOKED CHICKEN WITH RASPBERRY SAUCE

Serves 6

- ☐ **500 g (1 lb) pasta bows (farfalle)**
- ☐ **1.5 kg (3 lb) smoked chicken, flesh removed and cut into strips**
- ☐ **4 tablespoons slivered almonds, toasted**

SAUCE
- ☐ **250 g (8 oz) fresh or frozen raspberries**
- ☐ **3 tablespoons olive oil**
- ☐ **freshly ground black pepper to taste**
- ☐ **2 teaspoons sugar**
- ☐ **1 tablespoon lemon juice**

1   Cook pasta in boiling water in a large saucepan, following packet directions. Drain, set aside and keep warm.
2   To make sauce, place raspberries and oil in a food processor or blender and process until smooth. Place raspberry mixture, black pepper, sugar and lemon juice in a small saucepan. Bring sauce to the boil and simmer for 1 minute. Stir in chicken strips. Place pasta on a serving platter, pour chicken mixture over and sprinkle with almonds.

❖

STUFFED BREADSTICKS

Serves 4

- ☐ **1 breadstick, cut into 4 equal lengths**
- ☐ **24 small slices mozzarella**
- ☐ **24 slices salami**
- ☐ **24 slices tomato**
- ☐ **freshly ground black pepper**
- ☐ **2 tablespoons vegetable oil**

1   Make 6 slits in each length of breadstick, cutting almost all the way through.
2   Place a piece of cheese, salami and tomato in each slit. Sprinkle with black pepper and brush with oil.

3   Place under grill on medium heat until cheese melts and bread and salami are crisp.

❖

BLACKENED FISH

Serves 4

- ☐ **1 small onion, chopped**
- ☐ **1 tablespoon paprika**
- ☐ **$\frac{1}{2}$ teaspoon ground turmeric**
- ☐ **1 teaspoon chilli powder**
- ☐ **1 clove garlic, crushed**
- ☐ **1 tablespoon lime juice**
- ☐ **2 teaspoons grated fresh ginger**
- ☐ **1 tablespoon coconut milk**
- ☐ **4 fish cutlets**
- ☐ **1 tablespoon vegetable oil**
- ☐ **30 g (1 oz) butter**
- ☐ **lemon or lime juice**
- ☐ **steamed rice**

1   Place onion in a food processor and chop finely. Add paprika, turmeric, chilli powder, garlic, lime juice, ginger and coconut milk and process until well blended and smooth.
2   Coat each side of fish cutlets with paste. Heat oil and butter in a heavy-based frypan. Allow pan to heat for at least 5 minutes.
3   Place fish in pan and cook until blackened, on both sides. Serve with a squeeze of lemon or lime juice and steamed rice.

Smoked Chicken with Raspberry Sauce,
Stuffed Breadsticks, Blackened Fish

❖

POUSSIN WITH
RICE STUFFING

Poussins are young chickens reared for eating. For this recipe the birds should weigh about 375 g (12 oz) each.

Serves 4
Oven temperature 180°C, 350°, Gas 4

☐ **4 x 375 g (12 oz) poussins**
☐ **125 g (4 oz) butter, softened**
☐ **1 clove garlic, crushed**
☐ **2 tablespoons snipped fresh chives**
☐ **2 tablespoons chopped fresh parsley**
☐ **2 tablespoons oil**

STUFFING
☐ **185 g (6 oz) brown rice, cooked**
☐ **6 spring onions, finely chopped**
☐ **1 large avocado, stoned, peeled and mashed**
☐ **1 tablespoon lemon juice**
☐ **freshly ground black pepper**

1   Remove neck, and clean inside of birds, pat dry. Loosen skin over breast and tops of legs using fingers or the handle of a wooden spoon.
2   Mix butter, garlic, chives and parsley and spread under skin of birds.
3   For stuffing, combine rice, shallots, avocado and lemon juice. Season with black pepper and mix well. Fill birds' cavities with mixture. Tuck wings under body, tie legs firmly together and place in a baking tin. Brush with oil and bake for 30 minutes or until juices run clear when chicken are pierced with a skewer.

❖

RAINBOW RISOTTO

This savoury rice dish is enhanced by succulent pieces of colourful crisp vegetables.

Serves 4

☐ **1 tablespoon vegetable oil**
☐ **22 g (³/₄ oz) butter**
☐ **1 onion, chopped**
☐ **¹/₄ teaspoon ground turmeric**
☐ **410 g (13 oz) long grain rice**
☐ **1 litre (32 fl oz) vegetable stock**
☐ **1 small butternut pumpkin, peeled, seeded and chopped**
☐ **125 g (4 oz) fresh or frozen peas**
☐ **1 small red pepper, chopped**
☐ **2 courgettes, chopped**

1   Heat oil and butter in a large saucepan, cook onion and turmeric for 2-3 minutes. Stir in rice and stock, and bring to the boil. Reduce heat, cover and simmer for 15 minutes.
2   Boil, steam and microwave pumpkin and peas separately until tender. Drain and add to rice mixture with pepper and courgette. Cook for 4-5 minutes or until heated through.

Poussin with Rice Stuffing, Rainbow Risotto

FETTUCCINE WITH BLACK BEAN SAUCE

This East meets West type of dish uses Asian ingredients for the sauce and Italian pasta as the base. If you wish, in place of the fettuccine you could use Chinese noodles.

Serves 4

- ☐ **2 teaspoons oil**
- ☐ **1 clove garlic, crushed**
- ☐ **1 red chilli, seeded and finely chopped**
- ☐ **1 tablespoon canned black beans, washed, drained**
- ☐ **1 tablespoon soy sauce**
- ☐ **1 tablespoon vinegar**
- ☐ **1 tablespoon oyster sauce**
- ☐ **500 mL (16 fl oz) vegetable stock**
- ☐ **2 teaspoons brown sugar**
- ☐ **2 tablespoons cornflour blended with 4 tablespoons cold water**
- ☐ **500 g (1 lb) dried fettuccine**

1   Heat oil in a large frying pan, add garlic and chilli and cook for 1 minute. Combine black beans, soy, vinegar, oyster sauce, stock and sugar and cornflour mixture. Pour black bean mixture into pan, and simmer for 5 minutes, or until sauce thickens.

2   Cook pasta in boiling water in a large saucepan following the packet directions. Drain and place in serving dish. Toss through sauce and serve.

❖

TORTELLINI WITH SWEET RED PEPPER SAUCE

Serves 4

- ☐ **500 g (1 lb) tortellini**

SWEET RED PEPPER SAUCE
- ☐ **1 tablespoon oil**
- ☐ **1 onion, chopped**
- ☐ **440 g (14 oz) canned sweet red peppers, drained and chopped**
- ☐ **125 mL (4 fl oz) water**
- ☐ **1 tablespoon honey**
- ☐ **1 tablespoon chopped fresh oregano**

1   Cook tortellini in boiling water in a large saucepan, following packet directions. Drain, set aside and keep warm.

2   To make sauce, heat oil in small pan, add onion and cook for 3 minutes or until tender. Place red peppers, water, honey, oregano and onion in a food processor or blender and process until smooth.

3   Place sweet pepper sauce into a large saucepan and heat until simmering. Pour sauce over hot tortellini and serve.

PERFECT PASTA

The secret of perfect pasta is to bring a large saucepan of water to a rolling boil. Add a splash of oil to prevent sticking (do not add salt, as it toughens the pasta). Add the pasta and bring back to the boil, then cook 2-3 minutes for fresh pasta or 5-8 minutes for dried. Pasta should taste 'al dente' – just cooked but with no hard core in the centre. Drain and place in bowls, ready for the sauce.

Fettuccine with Black Bean Sauce, Tortellini with Sweet Red Pepper Sauce

Telephone Made Where Cushions Sandy de Beyer Plates Villeroy & Boch Fabric Signature

These desserts are truly indulgent,
ideal sweet treats for very special occasions.
Low- fat suggestions are included for
cholesterol watchers.

Sweet Tooth

❖

CHOCOLATE AND RUM
BREAD PUDDING

*An updated version of a traditional
recipe that is sure to be a hit with family
and friends.*

Serves 4
Oven temperature 150°C, 300°F, Gas 2

☐ **8 slices fruit loaf**
☐ **60 g (2 oz) butter, softened**
☐ **4 eggs, lightly beaten**
☐ **2 tablespoons caster sugar**
☐ **500 mL (16 fl oz) milk**
☐ **1 tablespoon rum**
☐ **1¹/₂ tablespoons powdered
   drinking chocolate**

1   Cut bread slices into 7.5 cm (3 in)
rounds using a pastry cutter, and butter
both sides. Place 2 bread rounds in the
base of four 375 mL (12 fl oz) ovenproof
dishes.
2   Combine eggs, sugar, milk, rum and 1
tablespoon of drinking chocolate and beat
until blended. Strain mixture over bread
rounds, then stand dishes in a baking
dish. Pour in enough water to come halfway
up sides of dishes. Sprinkle puddings with
remaining drinking chocolate and bake for
25-30 minutes or until firm.

❖

PANCAKES WITH
MARSHMALLOW SAUCE

Serves 4

SAUCE
☐ **75 g (2¹/₂ oz) butter**
☐ **90 g (3 oz) brown sugar**
☐ **125 mL (4 fl oz) double cream**
☐ **125 mL (4 fl oz) sour cream**
☐ **100 g (3¹/₂ oz) white marshmallows**
☐ **2 bananas, peeled and sliced**
☐ **ice cream (optional)**

PANCAKES
☐ **125 g (4 oz) self-raising flour**
☐ **3 eggs**
☐ **1 tablespoon caster sugar**
☐ **250 mL (8 fl oz) buttermilk**
☐ **22 g (³/₄ oz) butter, melted**

1   To make sauce, melt butter in a
saucepan. Stir in brown sugar and cook
over a low heat, stirring constantly without
boiling until sugar dissolves. Remove from
heat and blend in cream, sour cream and
marshmallows. Cook over a low heat,
stirring until smooth. Fold bananas into
mixture and set aside.
2   To make pancakes, sift flour into a
mixing bowl. Beat eggs and sugar together
until smooth. Add buttermilk and butter
and mix well. Blend egg mixture into flour
and mix until smooth.
3   Drop large spoonfuls of pancake
mixture into a heated, nonstick frying pan
and cook over a medium heat until golden
brown on both sides. Serve pancakes with
marshmallow sauce and ice cream (if
desired).

*Chocolate and Rum Bread Pudding,
Pancakes with Marshmallow Sauce,
Pear and Cheese Pastries (page 32)*

❖

PEAR AND CHEESE PASTRIES

Makes 16
Oven temperature 180°C, 350°F, Gas 4

- [ ] **8 sheets filo pastry**
- [ ] **45 g (1¹/₂ oz) butter melted**
- [ ] **4 tablespoons sugar**
- [ ] **2 pears, peeled, cored and sliced**

CHEESE FILLING
- [ ] **125 g (4 oz) blue vein cheese, (Danish Blue or Stilton) crumbled**
- [ ] **3 tablespoons ricotta cheese**
- [ ] **3 tablespoons chopped walnuts**
- [ ] **1 teaspoon ground cinnamon**
- [ ] **1 teaspoon finely grated lemon rind**

1 To make filling, place cheese, ricotta cheese, walnuts, cinnamon and lemon rind in a bowl and mix.

2 Brush 4 sheets of pastry with butter and sprinkle with a little sugar. Place on top of each other and cut into 10 cm (4 in) wide strips. Cut strips in half crossways. Place a pear slice on each strip. Top with a spoonful of cheese filling and roll up. Repeat with remaining pastry and pear slices.

3 Brush tops with remaining melted butter, sprinkle with remaining sugar and place on a greased oven tray. Bake for 15 minutes or until golden brown.

❖

TURKISH SYLLABUB

Serve this tangy dessert on its own in pretty glass dishes, or as a topping for fruit salad.

Serves 4

- [ ] **250 mL (8 fl oz) double cream**
- [ ] **1 tablespoon honey**
- [ ] **250 g (8 oz) natural yogurt**
- [ ] **1 tablespoon muscovado sugar**

Place cream and honey in a bowl and whip until thick. Fold in yogurt. Spoon into individual dishes, sprinkle with raw sugar and chill for 2-3 hours.

❖

HONEYDEW ICE

- ☐ **1 teaspoon gelatine**
- ☐ **2 tablespoons water**
- ☐ **1 small honeydew melon, peeled, seeded and chopped**
- ☐ **2 tablespoons lime juice**
- ☐ **2 teaspoons lime rind**
- ☐ **2 tablespoons honey**

1   Sprinkle gelatine over water in a cup, stand in a pan of hot water until it dissolves.
2   Place honeydew melon in a food processor or blender and process until smooth. Add gelatine mixture, lime juice, rind and honey whilst motor is running.
3   Pour mixture into a freezer container and freeze until just icy. Break up ice crystals with a fork, then return to freezer and freeze until set.
4   Place mixture in a food processor or blender and process until mushy. Serve immediately.

MICROWAVE IT

The gelatine can be dissolved in the microwave; cook on HIGH for 30 seconds or until gelatine dissolves.

❖

CAROB AND BANANA
ICE CREAM

This ice cream does not require beating during freezing and will keep indefinitely. It is delicious eaten on its own or served with fresh fruit.

Serves 4

- ☐ **6 large very ripe bananas, peeled and chopped**
- ☐ **250 mL (8 fl oz) vegetable oil**
- ☐ **2 tablespoons honey**
- ☐ **6 tablespoons milk powder**
- ☐ **250 mL (8 fl oz) water**
- ☐ **2 tablespoons carob powder**

1   Place bananas, oil, honey, milk powder, water and carob powder in a food processor or blender and process until smooth.
2   Pour into a freezerproof container, cover and freeze until firm.

Turkish Syllabub, Honeydew Ice, Carob and Banana Ice Cream

VITAMIN-RICH
YOGURT SUNDAE

Serves 4

☐ **750 g (1¹/₂ lb) natural yogurt**
☐ **250 mL (8 fl oz) concentrated blackcurrant syrup**
☐ **220 g (7 oz) canned unsweetened pineapple chunks, drained**
☐ **4 tablespoons wheatgerm**

1   Place 185 g (6 oz) yogurt in four tall dessert glasses.
2   Add 4 tablespoons blackcurrant syrup and 4 tablespoons pineapple to each glass and swirl to combine. Top each glass with 1 tablespoon wheatgerm and chill for 1 hour or until required.

CHERRY PEACH CRUMBLES

Serves 4
Oven temperature 180°C, 350°F, Gas 4

☐ **410 g (13 oz) canned stoned black cherries, drain and reserve 125 mL (4 fl oz) juice**
☐ **410 g (13 oz) canned sliced peaches, drain and reserve 125 mL (4 fl oz) juice**
☐ **2 teaspoons cornflour blended with 2 tablespoons cherry brandy**

TOPPING
☐ **45 g (1¹/₂ oz) macaroon biscuits, crushed**
☐ **1 tablespoon brown sugar**
☐ **2 tablespoons chopped flaked almonds**

1   Spoon cherries and peaches into four 250 mL (8 fl oz) ovenproof dishes. Place reserved juices and cornflour mixture in a saucepan and cook over a medium heat, stirring constantly, until sauce thickens slightly, then pour over fruit in dishes.
2   To make topping, combine macaroons, brown sugar and almonds. Sprinkle over fruit and bake for 10-15 minutes, or until heated through and golden brown.

Vitamin-Rich Yogurt Sundae,
Cherry Peach Crumbles

Glass and Scarf Made Where Plate and Bowl Villeroy & Boch

HONEY – THE MIRACLE FOOD

Honey is one of the oldest sweeteners known to man.

✧ In ancient times it was considered so valuable that it was used in place of gold to pay taxes.

✧ Greek athletes ate honey before entering the arena.

✧ Eros, the Greek god of love, dipped his arrows in honey.

✧ Honey keeps almost indefinitely; a jar found in an Egyptian tomb is estimated to be 3300 years old.

✧ Honey is one of nature's most powerful germ killers. Germs simply cannot survive in honey.

✧ Primitive man not only used honey as a food, but also to heal wounds.

✧ Honey can be used as a substitute for sugar in cooking. When using honey in place of sugar reduce the quantity of honey by a quarter and reduce the cooking temperature slightly to prevent overbrowning.

✧ Food sweetened with honey will have a better flavour if kept until the day after baking before serving.

✧ The ancient Egyptians used honey as a skin-care product.

✧ Honey when used on the skin opens clogged pores and helps balance moisture levels.

✧ When using honey as a skin-care product you should use unboiled honey, which should be available from health food shops.

✧ Natural unprocessed honey has been shown to increase calcium retention. It is also a good source of vitamin C, carotene and many of the B group vitamins.

✧ Sometimes you will find that honey crystallises on storage. If this occurs, place it in a pan of warm water until it liquifies, or heat in the microwave for a few seconds.

✧ Use honey as a sweetener for tea and herbal teas.

✧ As honey is a sticky product it can be hard to measure. To measure sticky liquid ingredients, such as golden syrup and honey, run the measuring utensils under boiling water for a few seconds before measuring. This will allow the liquid to run freely from the utensil. Or if packaged in glass jars, remove the lid and warm in the microwave on HIGH (100%) for 1 minute, then pour into your measuring utensil.

A sumptuous dinner that is sure to impress a special friend on a romantic occasion. Double the ingredients of the recipes and you have an elegant feast for four.

Dinner Date

MENU

- ◇ **Curried Pumpkin Soup**
- ◇ **Crusty Wholemeal Bread Rolls**
- ◇ **Cheesy Turkey Breast with Cherry Sauce**
- ◇ **Baby New Potatoes**
- ◇ **Strawberry and Kiwi Fruit Salad**
- ◇ **Chocolate Baskets with Berry Ice Cream**

❖

CURRIED PUMPKIN SOUP

A lightly spiced soup that takes less than half an hour to make. It can be made in advance and frozen or refrigerated, then reheated when you require it.

Serves 2

- ☐ **22 g (³/₄ oz) butter**
- ☐ **2 bacon rashers, chopped**
- ☐ **4 spring onions, chopped**
- ☐ **250 g (8 oz) butternut pumpkin, peeled and chopped**
- ☐ **750 mL (24 fl oz) chicken stock**
- ☐ **2 teaspoons curry powder**
- ☐ **2 teaspoons ground cumin**
- ☐ **2 teaspoons garam masala**
- ☐ **2 tablespoons sour cream (optional)**

1 Melt butter in a large saucepan, cook bacon and spring onions for 3 minutes. Add pumpkin, stock, curry powder, cumin, and garam masala. Cover, bring to the boil, reduce heat and simmer for 20 minutes, or until pumpkin is tender.
2 Place in a food processor or blender and process until smooth. Return to pan and heat through. Serve with a swirl of sour cream if desired.

❖

CHEESY TURKEY BREAST WITH CHERRY SAUCE

Serves 2

- ☐ **2 turkey breast fillets**
- ☐ **60 g (2 oz) Camembert cheese, sliced**
- ☐ **60 g (2 oz) butter**

CHERRY SAUCE
- ☐ **410 g (13 oz) canned stoned black cherries, drain and reserve 185 mL (6 fl oz) juice**
- ☐ **125 mL (4 fl oz) freshly squeezed orange juice**
- ☐ **3 tablespoons lemon juice**
- ☐ **1 tablespoon cornflour, blended with 3 tablespoons cold chicken stock or water**

1 Cut a slit in the side of each fillet, using a sharp knife. Fill cavity with Camembert slices and secure with toothpicks.
2 To make sauce, place cherries, reserved juice, orange and lemon juice and cornflour mixture in a saucepan. Cook over a medium heat, stirring constantly until mixture boils and thickens.
3 Melt butter in a frypan, cook fillets for 6-8 minutes, until golden brown. Remove toothpicks and top with hot cherry sauce.

❖

STRAWBERRY AND KIWI FRUIT SALAD

Serves 2

- ☐ **2 oak-leaf lettuce leaves**
- ☐ **125 g (4 oz) strawberries, hulled and halved**
- ☐ **1 kiwi fruit, peeled and sliced**

KIWI FRUIT VINAIGRETTE
- ☐ **1 kiwi fruit, peeled and puréed**
- ☐ **1 tablespoon vinegar**
- ☐ **2 teaspoons sugar**
- ☐ **ground black pepper to taste**

1 Fill lettuce leaves with strawberries and kiwi fruit.
2 To make vinaigrette, place kiwi fruit, vinegar, sugar, and pepper in a screwtop jar. Shake to combine. Spoon over fruit and serve.

❖

CHOCOLATE BASKETS WITH BERRY ICE CREAM

Serves 2

- ☐ **100 g (3 oz) dark chocolate, melted**

BERRY ICE CREAM
- ☐ **3 egg yolks**
- ☐ **5 tablespoons caster sugar**
- ☐ **315 mL (10 fl oz) double cream, whipped**
- ☐ **250 g (8 oz) fresh berries, such as raspberries, strawberries or blueberries**
- ☐ **2 tablespoons Frambois liqueur**

1 Allow chocolate to cool for a few minutes. Cover the outside of two lightly greased small bowls with plastic food wrap. Turn bowls upside down and place on a baking tray. Brush bowls with melted chocolate and set aside to set. Carefully remove chocolate cups from bowls and peel away plastic food wrap.
2 To make ice cream, beat egg yolks and sugar in a heatproof bowl over a saucepan of simmering water until pale and thick. Gently fold in cream and set aside.
3 Place berries and liqueur in a blender or food processor and process until smooth. Fold berry mixture into cream mixture and pour into a freezer container. Cover and freeze until firm. Place scoops of ice cream into chocolate baskets to serve.

Curried Pumpkin Soup, Cheesy Turkey Breast with Cherry Sauce, Strawberry and Kiwi Fruit Salad, Chocolate Baskets with Berry Ice Cream

Here's a stylish table for two that is easy and inexpensive to achieve. Items from an import emporium complement your favourite ornament centrepiece. We have also 'wrapped' our cushions especially for the occasion.

Orient Express

❖

TABLE FOR TWO

Our table measures 70 cm (32 in) square

MATERIALS
- ☐ **2 inexpensive bamboo and paper fans**
- ☐ **1 can black, high-gloss, spray paint (ozone-safe)**
- ☐ **small wicker basket for bread**
- ☐ **2 kg (4 lb) white plastic bucket (the sort that laundry powder comes in), for the ice bucket**
- ☐ **small white china pot for the candle**
- ☐ **1 disposable paper tablecloth (1170 x 1420 mm/47 x 57 in)**
- ☐ **1 candle**
- ☐ **ornament of your choice for centrepiece**
- ☐ **2 red paper napkins**
- ☐ **2 black paper napkins**
- ☐ **2 pieces fabric 75 cm (30 in) square**
- ☐ **2 pillow forms 30 x 30 cm (12 x 12 in)**
- ☐ **double-sided tape**
- ☐ **2 lengths of 2.5 cm (1 in) wide satin ribbon, each 1.10 m (44 in)**
- ☐ **toothpicks can be used to make fan 'stand'**

METHOD
1   Spray-paint open fans on one side. When completely dry, turn and paint other side. Set aside to dry. Spray-paint bread basket both inside and out. Leave to dry.
2   Wash and dry bucket thoroughly. Holding the can of paint upright, gently and quickly pass a spray of paint across bucket, to give a 'speckled' effect. Cover handle completely with paint. Spray china pot to match bucket. Set aside to dry.
3   To assemble, cover table with cloth, use fans as placemats and place cutlery. Melt wax at base of the candle, so candle will 'set' in the pot. Arrange centrepiece and flowers. Open out one red napkin and one black napkin. Placing black napkin on top of red one, hold napkins at centre and slip into a wine glass. Form points into a tulip shape.
4   Press under 5 cm (2 in) on two adjoining sides of fabric squares. Place pillow form in centre of wrong side of fabric. Fold fabric around pillow in an envelope style with pressed edges outermost. Secure with double-sided tape. Tie cushion with ribbon and tuck ends of ribbon under fold of fabric at back.

OTHER IDEAS
Choose colours to suit your decor and centrepiece. Colours can really complement your menu. You might like to choose cool colours for a relaxed seafood and salad meal, or a bold combination for a more stylish affair.
✧   Use linen, or linen and paper, instead of just paper napkins and cloth.
✧   Choose flowers to suit your colour choices. Anthurium, tiger lily or *strelitzia reginae* (bird of paradise flower) are dramatic and strong; whereas bud roses, baby's breath or freesias will create a different mood.

Choose colours to complement your decor to make this stylish but inexpensive Table for Two

Exercise is as important a part of your beauty routine as diet and skin care: regular exercise tones your body and gives a glow to your face; it makes you feel fit and trim – and when you feel good, you look good. As a bonus, exercise will reduce the risk of heart disease and osteoporosis in later life.

Workout

7 EASY WAYS TO WORKOUT

1 Walk wherever you can, instead of driving or taking a bus.

2 Walk up stairs – don't take the lift.

3 Hire an exercise bike; pedal while watching television or reading.

4 Take the dog for a walk every day.

5 Take regular short breaks whenever you are doing something sedentary to stretch and use inactive muscles.

6 Attack the housework with vigour and energy.

7 Go dancing at night; spend as much time as you can on the dance floor.

CHOOSING A SPORT

Whatever exercise you choose, the important thing is to do it regularly. You should find an activity that is convenient, enjoyable and can be maintained for 30 minutes or more as a continuous movement. Start at a careful level and build up activity gradually, as you develop stamina and condition. Some people find motivation easier if they join a fitness club or gym; others prefer to set the alarm half an hour earlier, slotting their exercise in first thing in the morning. Whichever way, make sure you tailor your exercise to your lifestyle and physical condition. If you are unfit, pregnant or have an existing medical condition such as heart or lung disease, check with your doctor before undertaking vigorous exercise.

OSTEOPOROSIS

While osteoporosis is a disease that occurs mainly in older people much can be done from an early age to prevent it. Osteoporosis is a reduction in bone density, this makes the bones more brittle and therefore more prone to fracture. It is believed that from about the age of forty, both women and men steadily lose calcium from their bones. However, osteoporosis is more common in women, than in men, because of the more rapid loss of calcium after menopause. You may prevent osteoporosis later in life by doing something now. The following are believed to have an influence on the rate of bone loss:

Exercise: If you do not already have a regular exercise programme start one. Remember you should start slowly

KILOJOULE (CALORIE)-BURNERS CHART

LIGHT	MODERATE	HEAVY	VERY HEAVY
10-20 kJ (2-5 Cals) burned per minute	**20-30 kJ (5-8 Cals) burned per minute**	**30-40 kJ (8-10 Cals) burned per minute**	**over 40 kJ (10 Cals) burned per minute**
Walking, slow	Walking, fast	Jogging	Swimming, training
Bowling, lawn or ten-pin	Gardening, heavy	Skipping	Squash, advanced
Golf	Tennis	Country dancing	Cross-country skiing
Table tennis	Bicycling	Disco dancing	Marathon running
Housework, light	Horseriding	Aerobics	Rowing
Gardening, light	Skating	Downhill skiing	Basketball
Yoga	Swimming, moderate	Netball	Uphill hiking
Water skiing	Ballroom dancing	Football	Fast bicycling
Painting	Sailing	Hockey	
Carpentry	Surfing	Climbing stairs	
Light industry	Hiking		
Assembly work			
Clerical work			

and work up to more strenuous exercise as you become fitter.

Calcium intake: Maintain a satisfactory intake of calcium throughout life. Ensure that you are including dairy products regularly in your diet. Choose the reduced-fat and modified low-fat milks; these have a richer taste than skim milk and have added calcium. They can also be used in place of regular milk in cooking.

Alcohol: When drinking wine with a meal, have a jug of iced water on the table as well. You will be surprised at how much longer that bottle of wine lasts and how much more you enjoy your food. A safe level of alcohol consumption is considered to be one to two drinks per day for women and three to four drinks per day for men.

Smoking: If you don't smoke, don't start; if you do, try to give up now.

Salt: Start cooking without salt. You will be surprised how quickly you get used to the 'new' taste. When buying canned and prepared products look for the low-salt and salt-free ones.

Caffeine: Try decaffeinated products. There is now a wide range of decaffeinated and caffeine-free coffee and cola products available.

Gym Gear The Physical Factory

42

When making natural skin-care products and herbal oils, you will need only basic kitchen equipment. Before you start there are a few methods and precautions that should be adhered to.

Practical Pointers

BASIC PROCESSES

Most recipes require either herb or flower water. The simplest herb water is made by steeping fresh or dried herbs in boiling water (infusion). However, the bark and roots of a plant will not yield their properties by this process and must be extracted by a method called a decoction; flowers need to be treated differently again.

❖

HERBAL WATER

This process uses the infusion method – if you need to make more just double the recipe. Herbal infusions can be made from one herb or a mixture of herbs, depending upon the requirements of a recipe or your particular needs.

Makes 250 mL (8 fl oz)

☐ **3-4 tablespoons fresh herbs or 1-2 teaspoons dried herbs**
☐ **250 mL (8 fl oz) boiling water**

Place the selected herbs in a large ceramic bowl and pour boiling water over them. Cover and steep for 12 hours, or as directed, then strain through muslin cloth and add required amount to the recipe.

Natural skin-care products are easy to make and all you need is basic kitchen equipment

❖

FLOWER WATER

This will give you beautifully scented water and can be made from any fragrant flower.

Makes 250 mL (8 fl oz)

☐ **4 tablespoons fresh flower petals**
☐ **375 mL (12 fl oz) water**

1   Place flower petals in a saucepan and cover with water. Bring to simmering point, cover and simmer for 30 minutes. Remove from heat, cool, strain through a muslin cloth, and squeeze any remaining liquid from the flower petals.
2   If necessary, and depending on the type of flowers used, repeat the process for greater potency, adding fresh flowers to the liquid and topping up with water if required.

❖

DECOCTION

Makes 125 mL (4 fl oz)

☐ **3-4 tablespoons fresh herbs or 1-2 teaspoons dried herbs**
☐ **315 mL (10 fl oz) water**

Place selected herbs in a stainless steel or enamel saucepan and add water. Bring to the boil and then gently boil for 30 minutes. Remove from heat, cover the pan and allow to steep for 10 minutes. Strain through a muslin cloth and add required quantity to recipe.

8 POINTERS TO PERFECT HOMEMADE COSMETICS

1   Do not use aluminium, metal, or nonstick pans for boiling or steeping herbs and flowers, or for the preparation of herbal recipes, as the metal may chemically react with the natural ingredients. Use only stainless steel or enamel pans for boiling, and ceramic or glass pots for steeping.

2   All equipment must be kept scrupulously clean, and preferably used only for the preparation of herbal recipes. This safeguards them from contamination by foodstuffs and other foreign substances. Always use a wooden spoon to stir, particularly when heating up ingredients.

3   Sterilise containers, including lids, in which you intend to keep cosmetics. Preferably use glass jars as they are easier to sterilise. Place glass jars and metal lids in a saucepan of water, bring to the boil, and allow to boil gently for 10 minutes. Remove from heat and leave containers in hot water until ready for use. Plastic containers and lids should be thoroughly scrubbed, rinsed with clean warm water, then filled with hot water and the lids replaced. Stand for 10 minutes, then invert the container and stand for a further 10 minutes.

4   Distilled water should be used in all recipes, as tap water contains chemicals and impurities which may interfere with the action of the herbs and other ingredients.

5   Adequately label everything you make – don't rely on memory.

6   An electric hand-held mixer can be used to homogenise the ingredients instead of beating with a spoon.

7   Herbal water and oils should be warm before adding to melted wax when making facial creams.

8   Whenever possible, always use fresh herbs unless dried herbs are specified. If using dried herbs, choose only those with good aroma and colour.

STORING HOMEMADE COSMETICS

✧ It is important to keep all herbal waters as fresh as possible. Being organic, and containing no preservatives, they will last only two or three days unless refrigerated. However, there are always exceptions such as lavender, which has good keeping qualities due to its antiseptic properties. Other infusions will keep quite well in a cupboard if blended with an odourless alcohol such as vodka, or a few drops of benzoin tincture.

✧ Infusions and shampoo preparations will keep from seven days to seven months in the refrigerator, provided that their containers have been sterilised. However, check them regularly to make sure they have not gone rancid.

✧ Lotions and creams made with lemon juice will keep for several weeks in a cool dark cupboard.

✧ It must be remembered that these preparations are not intended to be long-lasting like commercially manufactured cosmetics, therefore only small quantities are specified in the recipes.

ALLERGIC REACTIONS

✧ With so much pollution and ever-increasing stress in our daily lives, skin sensitivities and allergic reactions have greatly increased. Anyone, regardless of skin type, can be sensitive to a new substance, so no cosmetic can claim to be totally hypo-allergenic. It is therefore important to test any new substance or ingredient before use. Do this by placing a small amount of the preparation on the tender skin of your inner arm, between your elbow and wrist, and cover with a plaster. Leave for 24 hours, by which time any sensitivity will be evident.

✧ If skin reacts, stop using the preparation. If you can isolate the offending ingredient, replace it with a substitute or leave it out of the recipe altogether. Most herbs can be replaced with another; if the reaction is due to lanolin or glycerine, substitute beeswax.

MORE DOES NOT MEAN BETTER

As with all healing preparations, herbs can have very powerful effects, so always use the measurements given and never exceed the stated dose.

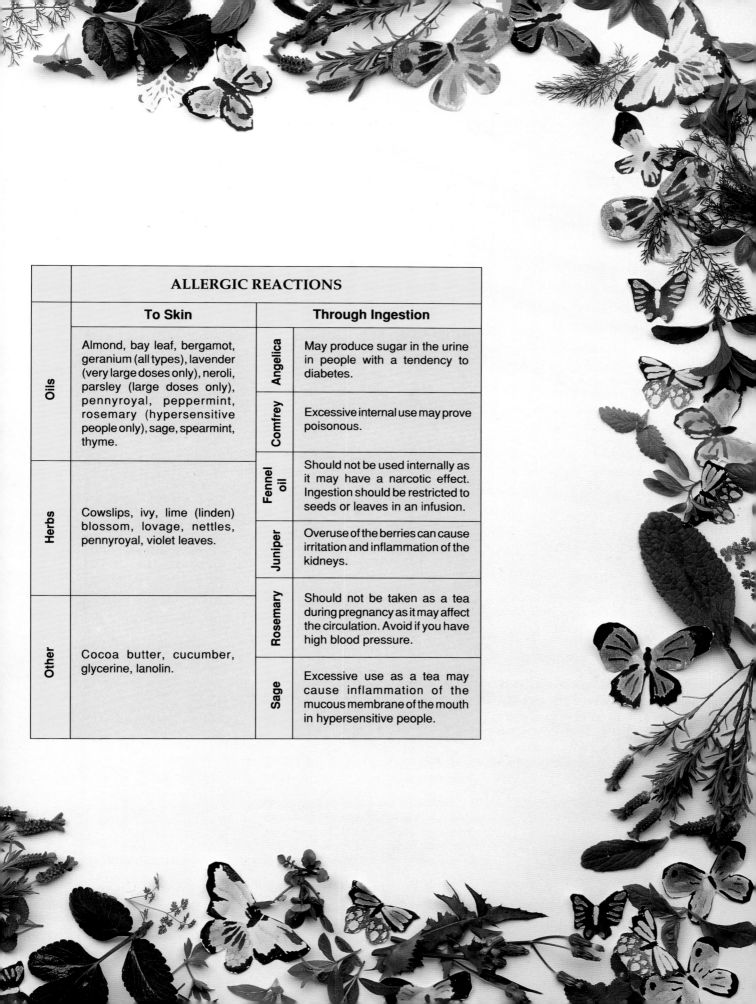

ALLERGIC REACTIONS

	To Skin		Through Ingestion
Oils	Almond, bay leaf, bergamot, geranium (all types), lavender (very large doses only), neroli, parsley (large doses only), pennyroyal, peppermint, rosemary (hypersensitive people only), sage, spearmint, thyme.	**Angelica**	May produce sugar in the urine in people with a tendency to diabetes.
		Comfrey	Excessive internal use may prove poisonous.
Herbs	Cowslips, ivy, lime (linden) blossom, lovage, nettles, pennyroyal, violet leaves.	**Fennel oil**	Should not be used internally as it may have a narcotic effect. Ingestion should be restricted to seeds or leaves in an infusion.
		Juniper	Overuse of the berries can cause irritation and inflammation of the kidneys.
Other	Cocoa butter, cucumber, glycerine, lanolin.	**Rosemary**	Should not be taken as a tea during pregnancy as it may affect the circulation. Avoid if you have high blood pressure.
		Sage	Excessive use as a tea may cause inflammation of the mucous membrane of the mouth in hypersensitive people.

Aromatherapy is the practice of using essential oils and resins extracted from flowers, plants and trees to restore vitality. These highly scented, volatile essences are plant hormones which can help renew and maintain good health.

The Art of Aromatherapy

ESSENTIAL OILS

Because of the small quantities of oil given up by plants and the high cost of purchasing them, it is not always practical to use a pure oil. Instead, their beneficial properties can be extracted with an odourless vegetable oil medium, which is suitable for scalp and body massaging.

❖

FRAGRANT MASSAGE OIL

☐ **fresh flower petals or fresh herbs**
☐ **soya oil**

Half fill a stainless steel or enamel pan with fresh flowers or herbs and cover with soya oil. Heat to 65°C, remove from heat, cool, strain, and store in airtight, dark-coloured glass bottles in a dark, cool spot.

KEEPING OILS

Essential oils should always be kept in small, dark-coloured, airtight bottles in a dark, cool spot. Never keep mixed oils any longer than two months, as they begin to oxidise as soon as the essential oils are blended.

❖

INHALATION

Steaming offers an effective method of treating many respiratory and sinus problems. Oils ideal for vaporising are peppermint and eucalyptus.

☐ **5 drops oil of your choice**
☐ **boiling water**

Half fill a ceramic bowl with boiling water, add oil, hold your face about 30 cm away and cover your head with a towel large enough to form a tent. Do not allow the vapour to escape. You should not steam your face for any longer than 10 minutes.

THE BENEFITS OF ESSENTIAL OILS

Essential oils are highly valued for the beneficial properties they exert upon the nervous system. Their fragrant perfumes calm, soothe, heal, fight infection, revitalise and relax. Use the appropriate combination of oils, whenever you need a lift, feel run-down, or cannot sleep.

❖

BATH OILS

Essential oils added to your bath release their special properties to penetrate your skin and exert their therapeutic value through the inhaled vapour. For maximum effect close all windows and the bathroom door.

☐ **fresh flowers or fresh herbs**
☐ **almond oil**

1 Half fill a stainless steel or enamel pan with fresh flowers or herbs and cover with almond oil. Heat to 65°C, remove from heat, cool, strain, and store in airtight, dark-coloured glass bottles in a dark, cool spot.
2 Add about 10 drops of oil to your bath while the taps are running, either singularly or in these combinations.

Variation
Bath oils can also be made by diluting 30 drops of essential oil with 2 tablespoons of almond oil.

❖

ROSEMARY AND LIME BATH OIL

Ideal for calming and relaxing you after a hard day.

☐ **2 drops rosemary oil**
☐ **4 drops lime flower oil**
☐ **2 drops bay leaf oil**
☐ **2 drops pennyroyal oil**

❖

CHAMOMILE BATH OIL

A relaxing and soothing oil which induces sleep.

☐ **6 drops chamomile oil**
☐ **2 drops lovage oil**
☐ **2 drops lime flower oil**

❖

ROSEMARY AND ROSE BATH OIL

Add this combination of oils to your bath to relieve tired and aching muscles.

☐ **2 drops rosemary oil**
☐ **2 drops rose oil**
☐ **2 drops bay leaf oil**
☐ **4 drops hyssop oil**

❖

ROSE BATH OIL

Helps to relieves stiffness after sport.

☐ **2 drops rose oil**
☐ **6 drops hyssop oil**
☐ **2 drops bay leaf oil**

❖

LAVENDER BATH OIL

When you need rejuvenating use this oil to give you back your bounce.

☐ **6 drops lavender oil**
☐ **2 drops lovage oil**
☐ **2 drops tangerine oil**

Inhalation, or steaming, is an effective way of treating many respiratory and sinus problems

Towel *Powder Blue* Jug and Basin Lifestyle Imports *Large Decanter* and *Shell Dish* Villeroy & Boch *Robe* Made Where *Makeup Bags* From Lois With Love

BATHING BEAUTIES

Choose from any of the following herbs and flowers according to your particular needs. Use herbs individually or in any combination that appeals.

Sweetly scents the skin	carnation, chamomile, clary, sage, eau-de-cologne mint, honeysuckle, jasmine, lavender, lemon balm, lovage, meadowsweet, orange flower, rose geranium, rosemary, rose, spearmint, violet	**Soothes, calms and relaxes**	bay leaves, chamomile, lemon balm, lime flowers, lovage, pennyroyal, valerian, yarrow
Softens the skin	chamomile, chickweed, comfrey, elder flower, fennel seed, marigold, marshmallow, orange flower, pansy, red clover, rose, sage, spearmint, violet	**Skin stimulants**	**Stimulating and tonic herbs** comfrey, dandelion, lovage, marjoram, nettles, rosemary, sage, savory, southernwood and lemon balm, thyme
For oily skin	**Astringent herbs that act on the sebaceous glands** clary, sage, comfrey, lemongrass, lemon verbena, lavender, peppermint, red clover, witch hazel	**As a skin tonic**	**Astringent and cleansing herbs** dandelion, horsetail, peppermint, red clover
To heal	elder leaves and flowers, plantain	**As a skin deodorant**	lovage, rosemary

❖

BATH OIL

Makes 600 mL (1 pt)

- ☐ **600 mL (1 pt) sunflower oil**
- ☐ **fresh herbs**

1   Fill a large, wide-mouthed jar with oil and then add as many of your chosen fresh herbs, in equal quantities, as it will take. Seal the jar and leave in a warm place for at least two days.
2   Strain mixture, squeeze any remaining oil from herbs, then repeat the procedure 10 more times.
3   Store in a tightly sealed bottle in a dark, cool place. Add 1 teaspoon of oil to the bath water.

HERBAL BATHS

Herbal baths are a luxury you can enjoy. They pamper and restore the body, soothe aching muscles, and gently calm the nerves. Fresh or dried herbs can be included as an infusion, as a bath oil or as a herbal vinegar, and will impart a delightful fragrance while they cleanse and beautify.

❖

BATH INFUSION

Makes 500 mL (16 fl oz)

- ☐ **155 g (5 oz) selected dried herbs**
- ☐ **500 mL (16 fl oz) boiling water**

Place herbs in a ceramic bowl and pour boiling water over them. Cover and allow to infuse for 1 hour, then strain through muslin cloth and add liquid to bath water.

❖

HERBAL BATH VINEGARS

Makes 500 mL (16 fl oz)

- ☐ **3 tablespoons selected dried herbs**
- ☐ **250 mL (8 fl oz) apple cider vinegar**
- ☐ **250 mL (8 fl oz) water**

1   Place dried herbs into a wide-mouthed glass jar. Heat together apple cider vinegar and water to just below boiling point. Pour the heated liquid over the herbs, seal tightly, steep for 12 hours and strain.
2   Add 250 mL (8 fl oz) vinegar to the bath water while the taps are running.

AROMATHERAPY MASSAGE

✧ Unlike therapeutic massage, aromatherapy uses smooth massaging strokes that have a firm, yet gentle pressure.

✧ Squeezing and vigorous hacking or slapping should be avoided, as the aim is to promote complete relaxation and allow easy penetration of the oil.

✧ The face, shoulders and neck will greatly benefit from this type of massage, leaving you with a feeling of vitality and wellbeing. Follow the directions described under massage, using the appropriate essential oil.

✧ If you choose not to make your own massage oil, dilute the neat essential oil in a carrier oil before use. Select a light, non-drying oil such as soya oil and add 3 per cent of your chosen essential oil to its total quantity.

BASIC WHITE SOAP

This soap contains pure vegetable oils and other natural products that will aid the complexion.

Makes 10 cakes

- ☐ **125 g (4 oz) caustic soda**
- ☐ **500 mL (16 fl oz) water**
- ☐ **750 mL (24 fl oz) coconut oil**
- ☐ **5 teaspoons castor oil**

1   Add caustic soda to water and stir until soda dissolves. The solution becomes hot, so set aside until it is lukewarm and then add oils. Stir for 2-3 minutes until all ingredients are well combined.

2   Pour into a shallow mould lined with damp calico, cover and leave for 24 hours to harden. Cut into cakes and store for 6 weeks before use.

MARSHMALLOW HERBAL WATER

If marshmallow is difficult to obtain you can replace it with dried marigold or rosemary.

Makes 500 mL (16 fl oz)

- ☐ **2 teaspoons dried marshmallow**
- ☐ **1 teaspoon dried fennel seed**
- ☐ **1 teaspoon dried chamomile**
- ☐ **500 mL (16 fl oz) boiling water**

Place marshmallow, fennel seeds and chamomile in a ceramic bowl and add boiling water. Cover and infuse overnight. Strain through a muslin cloth and use as required in recipe.

COSMETIC HERBAL SOAP

Makes 3 cakes

- ☐ **440 g (14 oz) grated basic soap**
- ☐ **410 mL (13 fl oz) Marshmallow Herbal Water**
- ☐ **155 g (5 oz) oatmeal**
- ☐ **75 g (2¹/₂ oz) honey**

1   Dissolve grated basic soap in herbal water over a medium heat. Add honey and oatmeal and mix well, stirring for at least 10 minutes. Remove from heat and pour into a large, shallow tray lined with damp calico.

2   Cover and leave for 24 hours to harden, after which time the soap can be used.

Herbal baths are a luxury you can enjoy. Herbal Bath Vinegars, Bath Oil and Cosmetic Herbal Soap will impart a delightful fragrance while they cleanse and beautify

Bottles Vasa Agencies

ROSEWATER AFTER-BATH BODY LOTION

This after-bath lotion will replace the natural oils lost through bathing and will leave your skin feeling luxuriously smooth and soft.

Makes 250 mL (8 fl oz)

- ☐ **125 mL (4 fl oz) rosewater**
- ☐ **1 teaspoon lemon juice**
- ☐ **2 teaspoons honey**
- ☐ **2 tablespoons almond oil**
- ☐ **4 drops essential oil of rose**
- ☐ **100 mL (3$^1/_2$ fl oz) glycerine**

1   Warm rosewater over low heat and stir in the lemon juice and honey until dissolved. Remove from heat, add the almond oil, rose oil and glycerine. Beat the mixture until it emulsifies.
2   Store in a sterilised, tightly capped bottle. Apply generously to the body after bathing, massaging well into the skin.

HERBAL TALCUM POWDER

What feels softer and smoother than talcum powder sprinkled on your skin after a refreshing bath or shower? This is an aromatic delight with mild deodorant properties and an elusive scent.

Makes 300 g (10 oz)

- ☐ **90 g (3 oz) French chalk**
- ☐ **45 g (1$^1/_2$ oz) cornflour**
- ☐ **4 g magnesium carbonate**
- ☐ **6 g calcium carbonate**
- ☐ **1 tablespoon orris root powder**
- ☐ **1 teaspoon essential oil of your choice**
- ☐ **3 teaspoons lovage water**

Mix French chalk, cornflour, magnesium carbonate, calcium carbonate and orris root powder together. Add essential oil and lovage water and mix until powder feels dry. Extra oil can be added if the scent is not strong enough, but take care not to allow the mixture to become too wet. If this does happen, adjust by adding more cornflour, a little at a time. Once dry, sieve twice and store in a plastic bottle with holes punched in its lid.

Use this range of natural cosmetics to leave your skin feeling smooth and soft after bathing

HERBAL DEODORANT

Natural deodorants do not inhibit perspiration, but control odours by preventing the growth of microorganisms.

Makes 750 mL (1$^1/_4$ pt)

- ☐ **6 tablespoons fresh lovage or spearmint**
- ☐ **3 tablespoons fresh rosemary**
- ☐ **cider vinegar**
- ☐ **distilled water**

1   Place lovage and rosemary in a bowl, add a little cider vinegar and bruise the herbs with the back of a spoon. Place in a large, wide-mouthed jar and pour over sufficient vinegar to just cover.
2   Seal jar tightly and place in a warm position. Leave for 14 days. Strain through a muslin cloth, squeeze any remaining vinegar from the herbs. Measure out the vinegar and for each teaspoon of vinegar add 2 tablespoons distilled water. Store in a tightly sealed bottle. To use, wash and dry under arms, dab on the vinegar and allow to dry.

Variation

If lovage or spearmint is unavailable use all rosemary instead.

BATH MITT

MATERIALS
- ☐ **piece towelling 25 x 45 cm (10 x 17³/₄ in)**
- ☐ **brown paper for pattern**
- ☐ **sewing thread**
- ☐ **15 cm (6 in) piece velcro**

METHOD
1 Cut towelling into three 25 x 15 cm (10 x 6 in) pieces. Stack towelling pieces on top of one another.

2 Place your hand on brown paper and roughly draw around it. Cut out shape leaving a straight edge at the wrist – this is the pattern for your mitt.

3 Cut three mitt shapes from towelling pieces. Fold 1 cm (¹/₂ in) in on straight edge of each mitt piece to the wrong side. Stitch down on one piece. Stitch velcro across two remaining folded raw edges on the wrong side. Press velcro strips together. Place mitt piece with hemmed edge over velcro trimmed pieces with right sides facing. Stitch around sides and top. Turn to right side.

Below: A towelling bath mitt is easy to make and a body scrub cleanses and softens your skin

Bottles Vasa Agencies

ALMOND MEAL BODY SCRUB

This body scrub is excellent for cleansing the body, softening the skin, and removing dead cells and hardened skin from elbows, knees and heels.

- ☐ **2 tablespoons almond meal**
- ☐ **2 tablespoons selected dried herbs**

Place almond meal and herbs in the pocket of a towelling bath mitt. Place glove over hand, and gently scrub your body while showering or bathing.

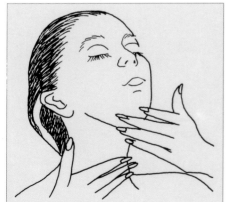

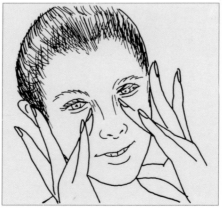

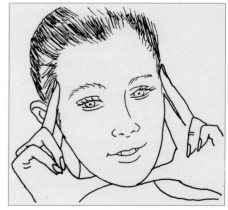

Give your face a treat, apply a light moisturiser and give yourself a facial massage.

Start at collar bone and brush fingers up neck and under chin. Roll knuckles over cheeks and gently roll skin between fingers until it tingles.

Position thumbs under chin and starting at inner corners of eyes run fourth finger gently over brow bone and down below eyes into corners again. Use a very light touch.

Place first and second fingers on temples and rotate firmly, without moving fingers, pressing as you go. Finish with a firm upward stroke along bridge of nose and forehead.

52

Your face is the mirror of your personality and one of the most expressive parts of your body. It is not hidden from view, so it is important to maintain natural beauty and take care of your skin. The foundation of a healthy complexion is diet and a sound skin-care routine.

Fresh Faces

SKIN TYPES

Normal: The skin is smooth, finely textured, soft and supple.

Dry: The skin is usually thin and delicate, often flaky, and prone to fine lines.

Oily: The skin is shiny and coarsely textured – often with enlarged pores – and prone to blackheads and spots.

Combination: This skin consists of both dry and oily areas. The oily skin usually forms a 'T' on the face – along the hairline, forehead, and a central strip down the face.

Sensitive: This skin is usually finely textured and often prone to reddish veins and patches. People with sensitive skins should stay away from stimulating herbs such as lavender, lime flower, mint, nettle, sage, southernwood and thyme.

Dull: The skin looks matt and lifeless, it has lost the bloom of vitality and the soft glow of renewal, and its acid balance has slipped.

Mature: The skin is a marvellous regenerative organ and, given the right encouragement, older skin can be toned, softened, and restored to much of its former beauty.

SKIN-CARE KNOW-HOW

Cleansing: Should be done once a day, preferably at night when the buildup of dirt is heaviest. If you have oily skin, cleanse again in the morning, as oil attracts dirt which adheres to it.

Toning: As cleansing opens the pores, it is important to use an astringent to close them. Toning also removes the last traces of grease, dead cells and grime.

Moisturising: A moisturiser will replace natural oils lost through cleansing and toning, keeping your skin supple and protecting it against moisture loss.

❖

FACIAL STEAM

A facial steam promotes perspiration, encourages the pores to expel impurities and dirt and leaves your face refreshed. A facial steam tends to dry the skin so only use once a week.

☐ **2 teaspoons selected dried herbs**
☐ **1 litre (1³/₄ pt) boiling water**

Place herbs in a ceramic bowl and add boiling water. Hold your face over the bowl and cover your head with a large towel, forming a head-tent. Steam your face and neck for about 10 minutes – no longer. After cleansing, apply a toner and moisturiser.

BEAUTY TIPS

If you suffer from asthma, difficulties in breathing, have dry skin that is sensitive to heat, or visible dilated veins, avoid a steam bath and use a face pack instead.

✧ For general cleansing and soothing use chamomile, lady's mantle, nettle, rosemary and thyme.

✧ For tightening facial pores use yarrow, peppermint and elder flower.

✧ As a skin healer use leek, comfrey or fennel.

✧ Vitamin C is essential for beautiful skin. It builds collagen and elastin, the bonding and structural substances that give your skin its tone and resilience.

6 EASY STEPS TO BEAUTIFUL SKIN

The basic steps for correct skin care are cleansing, toning and moisturising. However, before you start, the following simple rules should be remembered.

1   Do not overdo it – your facial skin is a living, breathing, eliminating and regenerative organ.

2   Be gentle when applying preparations – do not irritate or drag across your skin.

3   Smooth lotions on, then blot off excess after about 15 minutes.

4   Avoid extreme heat or cold – both are bad for your skin.

5   Clean your face regularly.

6   Do not clog the pores with make-up or heavy, rich moisturising creams.

❖

ELDER FLOWER AND SAGE FACE WASH

Wash your face morning and night with this herbal toilet water when not using a facial steam or mud pack. It will remove grime and help to keep the skin healthy and supple.

Makes 1 litre (1³/₄ pt)

☐ **4 tablespoons fresh elder flowers or 2 teaspoons dried elder flowers**
☐ **4 tablespoons fresh chamomile or 2 teaspoons dried chamomile**
☐ **4 tablespoons fresh rosemary or 2 teaspoons dried rosemary**
☐ **4 tablespoons fresh sage or 2 teaspoons dried sage**
☐ **1 litre (1³/₄ pt) boiling water**

Place elder flowers, chamomile, rosemary, sage and water in an enamel or stainless steel saucepan and boil for 30 minutes. Remove from heat, cool and strain through a muslin cloth. Store in a tightly sealed bottle in the refrigerator.

Variation

This face wash can also be made using just elder flowers or just rosemary.

CUCUMBER FACE MASK

A face mask helps to draw out grime from clogged pores. Its fine clay base acts as a light massage, balancing and revitalising the skin.

- ☐ **250 g (8 oz) fuller's earth**
- ☐ **¹/₂ peeled cucumber, pulped**
- ☐ **1¹/₂ tablespoons brewer's yeast**
- ☐ **olive oil**

Mix sufficient fuller's earth, cucumber pulp and juice, yeast and sufficient oil to make a thick paste. Apply to the face and neck, avoiding the area around your eyes and any broken skin. Leave on for approximately 10 minutes or until the mask feels tight. Remove with warm water and follow with a toner and moisturiser.

AVOCADO AND HONEY CLEANSER

Immediately after application the cleanser should be wiped off with a soft cloth, so that it is not absorbed.

Makes 125 mL(4 fl oz)

- ☐ **15 g (¹/₂ oz) beeswax**
- ☐ **22 g (³/₄ oz) anhydrous lanolin**
- ☐ **4 tablespoons avocado oil**
- ☐ **2 tablespoons rosewater**
- ☐ **2 teaspoons honey**
- ☐ **3 drops essential oil of rose**

1   Melt beeswax and lanolin in the top of a double boiler over a low heat. When completely liquid, stir in the avocado oil and rosewater and mix until well blended. Remove from heat, leaving top pan standing over hot water.
2   Stir in honey and oil of rose. Remove top pan from over hot water and beat vigorously until mixture is cooled and of a creamy texture. Store in a sterilised, screwtop jar.
3   To use, gently massage a small amount of cleanser into face, then remove all traces using a soft cloth.

AVOCADO MAKE-UP REMOVER

Makes 80 mL (2¹/₂ fl oz)

- ☐ **1 teaspoon dried sage or lemon verbena**
- ☐ **15 g (1 oz) beeswax**
- ☐ **4 tablespoons avocado oil**

1   Finely grind sage or lemon verbena in a pestle and mortar, or rub them through a fine sieve.
2   Melt wax in the top of a double boiler over a low heat. When wax is completely liquid stir in the avocado oil and ground herbs and mix until well blended. Remove from heat and beat the mixture until it has cooled. Store in sterilised, screwtop jars.
3   To use, massage a small amount onto face, then gently remove with a soft cloth.

CHAMOMILE AND MARIGOLD TONER

If you have a young healthy skin this is the toner for you.

Makes 500 mL (16 fl oz)

- ☐ **2 teaspoons dried chamomile**
- ☐ **1 teaspoon dried fennel seed**
- ☐ **2 teaspoons dried thyme**
- ☐ **1 teaspoon dried marigold petals**
- ☐ **500 mL (16 fl oz) boiling water**

1   Place chamomile, fennel, thyme and marigold petals in a ceramic bowl and add boiling water. Cover and allow to infuse overnight, then strain through a muslin cloth. Store in a tightly sealed bottle in the refrigerator for up to 10 days.
2   To use, apply by gently dabbing the solution onto the skin with a tissue, then leave to dry.

ROSEWATER INTENSIVE CREAM

Makes 185 mL (6 fl oz)

- ☐ **15 g (¹/₂ oz) beeswax**
- ☐ **1¹/₂ tablespoons almond oil**
- ☐ **1 tablespoon wheat germ oil**
- ☐ **2 tablespoons sunflower oil**
- ☐ **2 tablespoons rosewater**
- ☐ **1 teaspoon lemon juice**
- ☐ **2 drops essential oil of rose**

1   Melt wax, almond, wheat germ and sunflower oils in the top of a double boiler over a low heat. When mixture is completely liquid, stir in the rosewater and lemon juice and mix until well blended. Remove from heat, add rose oil and beat vigorously until cooled. Store in sterilised, screwtop jars.
2   To use, massage gently into face and neck morning and night.

10 TIPS TO HELP CONTROL ACNE

1   Try to avoid too much stress as this seems to cause acne.

2   Wash your face two or three times a day with a glycerine vitamin E soap, or with a soap designed specially for oily skin or acned skin.

3   After cleansing your face apply a refining lotion.

4   Treat trouble spots and blemishes with a medicated herbal compress.

5   Each morning after cleansing and refining, apply medicated herbal moisturising cream or ointment. This can also be dabbed onto trouble spots during the day and at night.

6   Do not pick at blemishes as this causes them to spread and leaves scars.

7   Make-up puffs, sponges or brushes that touch your face should be sterilised after each use.

8   Clean cotton wool is the best way to apply make-up.

9   Hair hanging over your forehead tends to aggravate acne.

10   Ensure a good calcium intake.

SAGE AND PEPPERMINT TONER

This toner will tighten enlarged pores, but it is not suitable for very sensitive skin.

Makes 250 mL (8 fl oz)

- ☐ **2 teaspoons dried sage**
- ☐ **1 teaspoon dried peppermint**
- ☐ **250 mL (8 fl oz) boiling water**

1   Place sage and peppermint in a ceramic bowl and add boiling water. Cover and allow to infuse overnight, then strain through a muslin cloth. Store in a sealed bottle in the refrigerator for up to 10 days.
2   To use, apply by gently dabbing the solution onto the skin with a tissue, then leave to dry.

Use this range of herbal products for a sound skin-care routine

❖

ALOE VERA FACE SCRUB

A face scrub has the same effects as a face mask, but it is faster. Just massage it in for a few minutes. This one is suitable for acne skin.

Makes enough for 1 face scrub

- [ ] **4 tablespoons fuller's earth**
- [ ] **2 tablespoons almond meal**
- [ ] **1 tablespoon finely ground dandelion**
- [ ] **1 tablespoon finely ground parsley**
- [ ] **1 tablespoon finely ground yarrow**
- [ ] **1 tablespoon finely ground chickweed**
- [ ] **1 teaspoon lemon juice**
- [ ] **1 tablespoon aloe vera juice**
- [ ] **2 teaspoons honey**
- [ ] **olive oil**

1 Mix together fuller's earth, almond meal, dandelion, parsley, yarrow, chickweed, lemon juice, aloe vera juice and honey. Add sufficient olive oil to form a thick paste.

2 Apply to face and neck, avoiding the area around your eyes and any broken skin. Massage lightly into skin for several minutes, then remove by rinsing thoroughly.

MARIGOLD FACE WASH

This herbal water will help blemishes. Use it when you are not using a face mask or acne scrub. It heals as well as restores the acid mantle to the skin.

Makes 2 litres (3¹/₂ pt)

- ☐ **4 teaspoons dried marigold petals**
- ☐ **2 teaspoons dried chamomile**
- ☐ **500 mL (16 fl oz) white wine vinegar**
- ☐ **witch hazel**
- ☐ **distilled water**

1 Place marigold petals and chamomile in a large, wide-mouthed bottle. Gently warm vinegar, pour it over herbs.
2 Tightly seal the bottle, then place in a warm place and leave to infuse for 2 weeks.
3 Strain through a muslin cloth. Repeat procedure if the scent is not strong enough.
4 Measure vinegar mixture and for each 1 tablespoon of mixture add 1 tablespoon witch hazel and 125 mL (4 fl oz) distilled water. Store in tightly sealed, sterilised bottles.

MARIGOLD REFINING LOTION

If you suffer from problem skin, use this refining lotion, instead of a skin toner. Apply after cleansing.

Makes 300 mL (9¹/₂ fl oz)

- ☐ **1 teaspoon dried marigold petals**
- ☐ **250 mL (8 fl oz) boiling water**
- ☐ **witch hazel**

1 Place marigold petals in a ceramic bowl and add boiling water. Cover and allow to infuse overnight, then strain through a muslin cloth.
2 Measure lotion and for each 3 tablespoons add 1 tablespoon witch hazel. Store in a tightly sealed bottle in the refrigerator for up to 10 days.

FACE SAVER
Never use fingernails to remove blackheads. Use two cotton buds to gently push the surrounding skin until you dislodge the blackhead.
✧ An easy way of treating spots and blemishes is to apply a herbal compress to the problem areas.

MARIGOLD AND CHAMOMILE INFUSION

Makes 500 mL (16 fl oz)

- ☐ **2 teaspoons dried marigold**
- ☐ **2 teaspoons dried chamomile**
- ☐ **500 mL (16 fl oz) boiling water**

1 Place marigold petals and chamomile in a ceramic bowl and pour over boiling water. Cover and allow to infuse overnight, then strain through a muslin cloth and store in sterilised bottles in the refrigerator for up to 10 days.
2 To use, heat infusion to lukewarm. To make a compress, dip sterile gauze or cotton wool into warm infusion and hold against affected area of skin for 15 minutes.

DANDELION AND PARSLEY INFUSION

Make this infusion into a compress and apply to blackheads.

Makes 250 mL (8 fl oz)

- ☐ **15 g (¹/₂ oz) dried dandelion leaves**
- ☐ **2 teaspoons fresh parsley**
- ☐ **2 teaspoons dried yarrow**
- ☐ **500 mL (16 fl oz) water**

1 Place dandelion leaves, parsley and yarrow in a ceramic bowl, add water. Cover and allow to infuse overnight, then strain through a muslin cloth and store in sterilised bottles in the refrigerator for up to 10 days.
2 To use, heat infusion to lukewarm. To make a compress, dip sterile gauze or cotton wool into warm infusion and hold against affected area of skin for 15 minutes.

LEMONGRASS AND HONEY MOISTURISER

Replaces natural oils and helps treat acne.

Makes 75 g (2¹/₂ oz)

- ☐ **15 g (¹/₂ oz) beeswax**
- ☐ **1¹/₂ tablespoons almond oil**
- ☐ **1 tablespoon wheat germ oil**
- ☐ **2 tablespoons lemongrass oil**
- ☐ **2 tablespoons Lemongrass Herbal Water**

- ☐ **1 teaspoon lemon juice**
- ☐ **2 teaspoons honey**

Melt wax and almond, wheat germ and lemongrass oils in the top of a double boiler over a low heat. When wax is completely liquid, stir in herbal water and lemon juice. Remove from heat, keeping the top pan standing over the hot water. Add honey and stir until well blended, then remove the top pan and set aside to cool. Beat mixture until thick and creamy.

LEMONGRASS HERBAL WATER

- ☐ **2 teaspoons dried lemongrass**
- ☐ **2 teaspoon dried marigold petals**
- ☐ **boiling water**

Place lemongrass and marigold petals in a ceramic bowl. Add enough boiling water to cover leaves. Place a towel or plate on the bowl and set aside to infuse overnight, then strain through a muslin cloth and use as required.

OCCASIONAL PIMPLES
Occasional pimples are a nuisance, unsightly, and always appear when you least want them to. The following treatment is quick and easy, and will heal a pimple overnight.
✧ Bruise a fresh marigold (calendula) petal and then gently, but firmly, press it onto the affected spot for 2 to 3 minutes. Repeat the application from time to time. In the morning there will be just a trace of redness. However, this will completely disappear in a few hours if the procedure is repeated one more time.
✧ If a fresh marigold petal is not available, you can use a fresh marigold leaf in the same way.

Washing and conditioning your hair with herbal preparations will leave it shiny and manageable

Beautiful, shiny hair is one of your greatest
beauty assets. Regular washing and conditioning
with herbs will leave your hair healthy,
shiny and manageable.

Healthy Hair

Vase, Soap Dish and Dispenser Martinvale Headband From Lois With Love Mirror Mosmania Towel Powder Blue Blanket Made Where

SHAMPOO HERBS

Catmint: Promotes hair growth and adds a shine to dry-looking hair.

Chamomile: Ideal for fair hair as it has a lightening effect. Healing to scalp irritations.

Comfrey: Has a soothing and healing effect on scalp irritations.

Elder flower: Gentle stimulant to the hair.

Horsetail: Stimulates hair growth; cleansing, astringent for oily hair.

Lemon balm: Gently cleanses; imparts a spicy lemon scent to the hair.

Lemongrass: Cleansing and astringent.

Lemon verbena: Fragrant cleansing herb and pore stimulant.

Nettle: Gently cleanses the hair and stimulates scalp circulation.

Parsley: Healing to scalp conditions, stimulates the hair follicles and balances sebaceous glands.

Rosemary: Ideal for deeper shades of hair colour; helps control dandruff.

Sage: Astringent for oily hair and is ideal for dark hair.

Thyme: Cleansing, astringent and tonic.

Yarrow: Refreshing and cleansing; acts as a tonic for the hair.

CONDITIONING RINSES

Place the herbs of your choice in a ceramic bowl and pour boiling water over them. Cover and allow to infuse overnight, then strain through a muslin cloth. Store in a suitable tightly corked container in the refrigerator for up to 7 days.

✧ To use, hold your head over a large bowl and pour the rinse several times over wet hair immediately after shampooing. Choose the herbs that best suit your hair and skin type.

To add shine to dark hair: Parsley, red sage or rosemary

Fair hair: Chamomile, yarrow or marigold

To lighten fair hair: Use a strong infusion of chamomile

To darken dark hair: Red sage – steep for 24 hours and add black tea.

These easy-to-make hair care products will add extra bounce to your hair

❖

SCALP MASSAGING OIL

Makes 375 mL (12 fl oz)

- ☐ **30 g (1 oz) fresh chamomile for fair hair or fresh red sage for dark hair**
- ☐ **22 g (³/₄ oz) fresh rosemary**
- ☐ **22 g (³/₄ oz) fresh peppermint**
- ☐ **600 mL (1 pt) soya oil**

1 Place chamomile or sage, rosemary and peppermint in a wide-mouthed jar. Add soya oil. Seal and leave in a warm place for 2 days.

2 Strain mixture, squeezing any remaining oil from herbs. Add fresh herbs and repeat the procedure 10 more times. Store in a corked glass bottle in a dark, cool spot.

3 To use, massage a small amount of oil into your scalp after shampooing.

❖

ALMOND OIL PRE-WASH CONDITIONER

Your scalp will dry out unless you treat it with a moisturising oil. This conditioner will protect your skin by replacing natural surface oils.

Makes 250 mL (8 fl oz)

- ☐ **250 mL (8 fl oz) almond oil**
- ☐ **2 tablespoons fresh peppermint**
- ☐ **1 tablespoon fresh thyme**

1 Pour almond oil into a suitable wide-mouthed bottle and add peppermint and thyme. Seal tightly and place bottle in a warm place for at least 14 days.

2 Strain, squeeze out the herbs, and repeat the procedure with a fresh batch of herbs. Store in an airtight container.

❖
HERBAL SHAMPOO

The following recipe is the basis for your own natural shampoo. It can be tailored to suit your particular needs.

Makes 250 mL (8 fl oz)

- ☐ **250 mL (8 fl oz) Soapwort Herbal Water**
- ☐ **2 teaspoons liquid coconut oil**
- ☐ **1 teaspoon glycerine**

Place herbal water, coconut oil and glycerine in a bowl and mix until well blended. Store in a suitable plastic bottle.

❖
SOAPWORT HERBAL WATER

Makes 600 mL (1 pt)

- ☐ **4¹/₂ tablespoons fresh herbs of your choice (see list for those suitable for your hair)**
- ☐ **1 handful fresh soapwort leaves and stems, or 2 tablespoons dried soapwort**
- ☐ **600 mL (1 pt) boiling water**

1 Place herbs and soapwort in a ceramic bowl and add boiling water. Cover and infuse overnight, then strain through a muslin cloth.
2 Add required amount to shampoo recipe – any leftover can be used in the bath.

Bottles Vasa Agencies

11 STEPS TO BEAUTIFUL HAIR

Although herbs provide a good foundation for beautiful hair, the way you care for it is important too.

1 After washing your hair, dry it naturally. Sit back and relax in the sun while you gently flick the moisture out with your fingertips, or loosely wrap it in a towel until it dries.

2 Wash your hair only when necessary. If you wash it too frequently it can overstimulate the scalp and produce dry, brittle ends.

3 Use a pre-wash conditioner before shampooing to take care of dry ends.

4 Always wet hair thoroughly with warm water before applying shampoo.

5 Rinse out all traces of shampoo and conditioner before drying your hair.

6 Do not brush wet hair or you will split the ends and pull the hair out by the roots. Use a wide-toothed comb.

7 Avoid using a dryer, especially on dripping wet hair. If you must use one, towel-dry the hair first and then put the dryer on a warm or cool setting. Excessive use of curling tongs and heated rollers will dry out your hair and make it brittle.

8 Do not brush hair excessively or tease it, as these treatments will aggravate brittle and oily hair conditions. If you must tease your hair, start at the roots and do it in sections.

9 Always keep your brushes and combs scrupulously clean. Wash them in a diluted rosemary decoction to eliminate grease build-up.

10 Have your hair cut about every six weeks to keep the style in shape and to get rid of split ends.

11 After swimming in salt or chlorinated water, wash your hair with a herbal shampoo and then rinse with a chamomile conditioner.

Bright Eyes

❖

MORNING EYE CREAM

A gentle cream that will smooth, soothe and moisturise the delicate tissue surrounding your eyes.

Makes 300 g (9$\frac{1}{2}$ oz)

☐ **100 g (3$\frac{1}{2}$ oz) pure lanolin**
☐ **200 g (6$\frac{1}{2}$ oz) castor oil**

1   Place lanolin and oil in a saucepan and melt over a low heat. Remove from heat and pour into a sterilised, screwtop jar. Allow to cool before sealing.
2   To use, massage a small amount into skin around the eyes after cleansing.

❖

PARSLEY AND CHAMOMILE EYE COMPRESS

Always make a fresh infusion for each treatment.

☐ **fresh parsley**
☐ **fresh chamomile flowers**
☐ **boiling water**

1   Place parsley and chamomile flowers in a ceramic bowl. Add enough boiling water to cover the herbs, then cover and leave to infuse until tepid.
2   Moisten two pads of cotton wool with the infusion, lie down, and place one over each eye and relax for 10-15 minutes. Make sure the cotton wool is not so wet that the liquid runs into your eyes.

❖

PARSLEY AND FENNEL EYE COMPRESS

The herbal infusion used for this compress relieves tired and bloodshot eyes.

☐ **6 tablespoons chopped fresh parsley**
☐ **1 teaspoon dried fennel seeds**
☐ **2 teaspoons dried chamomile**
☐ **boiling water**

1   Place parsley, fennel seeds and chamomile in a ceramic bowl. Add enough boiling water to cover the herbs, then cover and leave to infuse until tepid.
2   Moisten two pads of cotton wool with the infusion, lay down, and place one over each eye and relax for 10-15 minutes. Make sure the cotton wool is not so wet that the liquid runs into your eyes.

FACE SAVER

When applying any creams to the eye area always work away from the eyes.
✧   For a quick eye-brightener, cut a slice of cucumber and rub this over the eyelid and the skin below the eye. Close your eyes for a couple of minutes to allow the juice to dry. Then pat on – do not rub in – a minute drop of wheat germ oil.

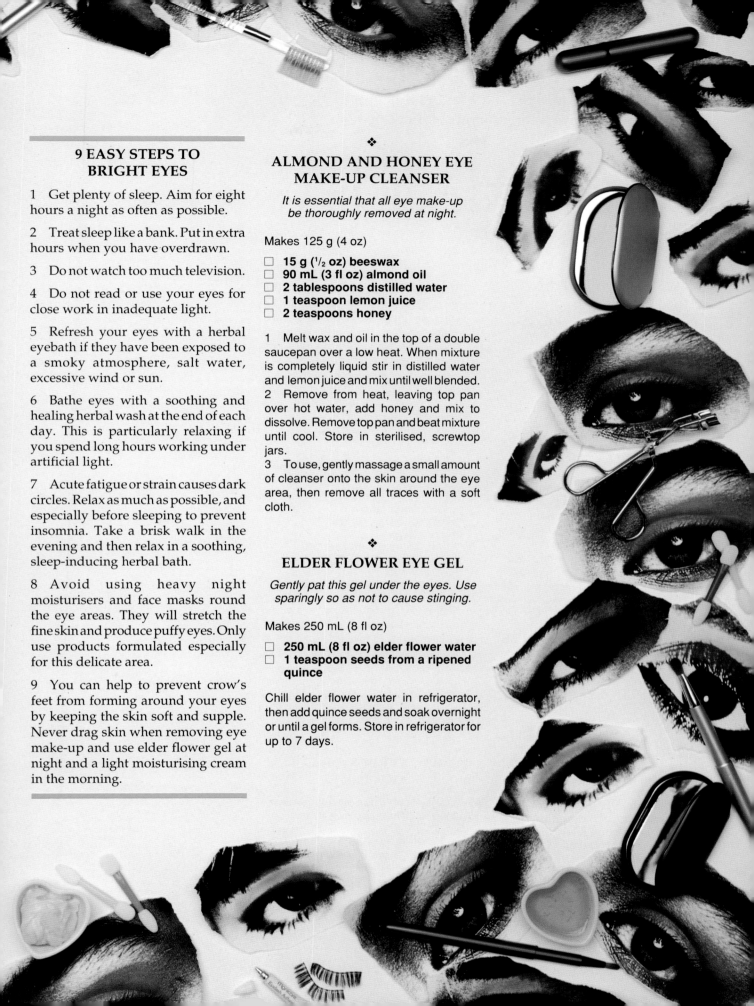

9 EASY STEPS TO BRIGHT EYES

1 Get plenty of sleep. Aim for eight hours a night as often as possible.

2 Treat sleep like a bank. Put in extra hours when you have overdrawn.

3 Do not watch too much television.

4 Do not read or use your eyes for close work in inadequate light.

5 Refresh your eyes with a herbal eyebath if they have been exposed to a smoky atmosphere, salt water, excessive wind or sun.

6 Bathe eyes with a soothing and healing herbal wash at the end of each day. This is particularly relaxing if you spend long hours working under artificial light.

7 Acute fatigue or strain causes dark circles. Relax as much as possible, and especially before sleeping to prevent insomnia. Take a brisk walk in the evening and then relax in a soothing, sleep-inducing herbal bath.

8 Avoid using heavy night moisturisers and face masks round the eye areas. They will stretch the fine skin and produce puffy eyes. Only use products formulated especially for this delicate area.

9 You can help to prevent crow's feet from forming around your eyes by keeping the skin soft and supple. Never drag skin when removing eye make-up and use elder flower gel at night and a light moisturising cream in the morning.

❖

ALMOND AND HONEY EYE MAKE-UP CLEANSER

It is essential that all eye make-up be thoroughly removed at night.

Makes 125 g (4 oz)

- ☐ **15 g (¹/₂ oz) beeswax**
- ☐ **90 mL (3 fl oz) almond oil**
- ☐ **2 tablespoons distilled water**
- ☐ **1 teaspoon lemon juice**
- ☐ **2 teaspoons honey**

1 Melt wax and oil in the top of a double saucepan over a low heat. When mixture is completely liquid stir in distilled water and lemon juice and mix until well blended.
2 Remove from heat, leaving top pan over hot water, add honey and mix to dissolve. Remove top pan and beat mixture until cool. Store in sterilised, screwtop jars.
3 To use, gently massage a small amount of cleanser onto the skin around the eye area, then remove all traces with a soft cloth.

❖

ELDER FLOWER EYE GEL

Gently pat this gel under the eyes. Use sparingly so as not to cause stinging.

Makes 250 mL (8 fl oz)

- ☐ **250 mL (8 fl oz) elder flower water**
- ☐ **1 teaspoon seeds from a ripened quince**

Chill elder flower water in refrigerator, then add quince seeds and soak overnight or until a gel forms. Store in refrigerator for up to 7 days.

Your hands are among the hardest worked parts
of your body and accordingly deserve special attention.
They are always on show – therefore, it is important that
they always look good and function well.

Soft Hands

❖

ELDER FLOWER HAND CREAM

Use a little of this cream on dry hands.

Makes 125 g (4 oz)

- ☐ **15 g (¹/₂ oz) beeswax**
- ☐ **15 g (¹/₂ oz) glycerine**
- ☐ **1 tablespoon wheat germ oil**
- ☐ **2 teaspoons jojoba oil**
- ☐ **1¹/₂ tablespoons almond oil**
- ☐ **1¹/₂ tablespoons olive oil**
- ☐ **2 tablespoons elder flower water**
- ☐ **1 teaspoon lemon juice**

1   Melt beeswax and glycerine in the top of a double boiler over a low heat. When completely liquid stir in wheat germ, jojoba, almond and olive oils, elder flower water and lemon juice.
2   Remove from heat and beat mixture vigorously until cool and of a creamy texture. Store in sterilised, screwtop jars.

❖

ELDER FLOWER INTENSIVE CARE REPAIR CREAM

This cream will alleviate mild damage and moisturise the skin.

Makes 125 g (4 oz)

- ☐ **15 g (¹/₂ oz) beeswax**
- ☐ **30 g (1 oz) lanolin**
- ☐ **1 tablespoon witch hazel**
- ☐ **1 tablespoon elder flower water**
- ☐ **7 teaspoons almond oil**
- ☐ **1¹/₂ tablespoons wheat germ oil**
- ☐ **2 teaspoons sunflower oil**
- ☐ **1 teaspoon lemon juice**
- ☐ **6 drops of essential oil of fennel**
- ☐ **10 drops of essential oil of marigold**

1   Melt wax and lanolin in the top of a double boiler over a low heat. When mixture is completely liquid stir in witch hazel and elder flower water, almond, wheat germ and sunflower oils and lemon juice and mix well.
2   Remove from heat, add essential oil of fennel and essential oil of marigold, and beat vigorously until cool. Store in a sterilised, screwtop jar.

❖

PROTECTIVE HAND CREAM

Makes 125 g (4 oz)

- ☐ **5 teaspoons lanolin**
- ☐ **3 teaspoons glycerine**
- ☐ **5 g beeswax**
- ☐ **75 mL (2¹/₂ oz) safflower oil**
- ☐ **2 tablespoons Lemon Verbena Herbal Water**
- ☐ **3 teaspoons fresh lemon juice**

1   Melt lanolin, glycerine and beeswax in the top of a double boiler over a low heat. When mixture is completely liquid stir in the safflower oil and herbal water and mix until well blended.
2   Remove from heat, add lemon juice and beat vigorously until cool. Store in sterilised, screwtop jars.

❖

LEMON VERBENA HERBAL WATER

- ☐ **3 teaspoons dried lemon verbena**
- ☐ **250 mL (8 fl oz) boiling water**

Place lemon verbena in a ceramic bowl and add boiling water. Allow to steep overnight, then strain through a muslin cloth and use as required.

Your hands are always on show and deserve special attention

Small Containers and Mirror Made Where Jug and Basin Martinvale Towel Powder Blue

10 WAYS TO BEAUTIFUL HANDS

1 Apply a protective barrier cream before commencing rough work, washing up or messy household jobs.

2 Use protective gloves for gardening and household chores.

3 Avoid direct contact with chemical cleansers.

4 Apply a good herbal moisturising hand cream morning and night.

5 Wear natural fibre gloves, such as wool, when out in cold weather.

6 Use a natural skin repair cream whenever hands have suffered excessive exposure to salt water, sun, wind; or when signs of roughening, chapping and cracking appear.

7 To help your body assimilate calcium, and give you strong, healthy fingernails, you need a rich source of silica. Nature's best sources are the herb horsetail (*Equisetum arvense*), borage flowers, dill seed, and chives.

8 To maintain your nails in tip top condition, check your diet: helpful foods are barley, kelp, garlic, onion, parsley, rice, chives, celery, lettuce and sunflower seeds.

9 Include a regular nail bath and herbal tea, rich in silicon, in your weekly health routine.

10 To keep fingernails supple, massage a little olive oil into them each night after the herbal finger bath.

❖

NAIL BATH

☐ **3 teaspoons dried horsetail**
☐ **3 teaspoons dried dill seeds**
☐ **250 mL (8 fl oz) boiling water**

1 Place horsetail and dill seeds in a ceramic bowl and add boiling water. Cover and allow to infuse overnight, then strain through a muslin cloth. Store in a glass bottle in the refrigerator for up to 7 days.
2 To use, soak fingertips in the infusion morning and night for 15 minutes.

Most foot problems are caused by badly fitting shoes or lack of foot care. So do your feet a favour and give them the attention they deserve.

Footwork

❖

ALMOND FOOT MASSAGE OIL

If you haven't time for a foot bath, massage this oil into tired and aching feet. It can also be used after soaking.

Makes 500 mL (16 fl oz)

- ☐ **250 mL (8 fl oz) almond oil**
- ☐ **250 mL (8 fl oz) Herbal Oil (see recipe)**

Mix together almond oil and Herbal Oil. Pour into a suitable glass bottle, seal, and store in a dark cool place until required.

9 WAYS TO BETTER FEET

1 Let your feet breathe. Walk barefoot as often as possible to let your feet recover from the confinement of shoes.

2 When out-of-doors and during leisure time wear sensible footwear: flat-heeled, comfortable, open leather shoes or sandals are the best.

3 Do not wear nylon stockings unless absolutely essential.

4 Choose shoes with heels less than 5 cm (2 in) high, and try to wear different shoes each day.

5 Shop for shoes in the afternoon, as your feet swell during the day.

6 Make sure your shoes are at 2.5 cm (1 in) longer than your toes.

7 Avoid buying plastic shoes. Choose leather or fabric shoes as these will allow your feet to breathe.

8 Avoid wearing tight boots for long periods as they tend to restrict circulation.

9 If you must wear close-fitting shoes sprinkle a little powdered, dry chamomile flowers, peppermint leaves, pennyroyal or hyssop inside them.

❖

HERBAL OIL

Use this Herbal Oil when making the Almond Foot Massage Oil. It can also be used as a body massage oil.

☐ **fresh rosemary**
☐ **fresh marigold**
☐ **almond oil**

Place rosemary and marigold in a stainless steel or enamel pan, cover with almond oil and heat to 65°C (165°F). Remove from heat, cool, strain, and use as required.

❖

SOOTHING ROSEMARY FOOT BATH

Tired feet give you a tired-looking face, so at the end of a busy day soak your feet in an invigorating and soothing foot bath.

☐ **2 tablespoons dried bay leaf**
☐ **3 tablespoons fresh plantain leaves**
☐ **3 tablespoons fresh rosemary**
☐ **2 tablespoons fresh angelica**
☐ **3 tablespoons fresh lovage**
☐ **boiling water**
☐ **1 tablespoon sea salt**

1 Place bay leaves, plantain leaves, rosemary, angelica and lovage in a bowl and pour boiling water over them. Cover and allow to infuse for 30 minutes, then strain and discard herbs.
2 Bring liquid to the boil in a stainless steel or enamel pan, then pour into a bowl large enough for your feet. Stir in salt until it dissolves, leave to cool slightly then soak your feet. After soaking, revive your feet with a quick dip in cold water.

FEET FIRST

Try this simple foot exercise to firm muscles and help feet recover from the confinement of shoes. Gently stretch the arch and curl toes underneath. Hold this position and count to ten. Repeat three times with each foot when you are sitting down.

✧ To treat corns, rub each night with a crushed garlic clove, or put a sliver of garlic on the corn and hold it in place with a plaster. Or apply fresh, crushed marigold leaves to the corn morning and night.

✧ Feet cannot be elegant with a fungus infection in residence between your toes. To alleviate the problem try the following: an application of cider vinegar, or a poultice of red clover flowers – boiled first to soften them.

✧ At the end of a busy day give your feet a treat – put them into a relaxing foot bath. Afterwards, generously massage them with a soothing and healing herbal foot oil.

✧ Give your feet a regular pedicure. Always cut toenails straight across.

Towel Powder Blue Bottle *(far left)* Villeroy & Boch

A good massage is an effective drugless therapy that enhances circulation and improves skin and muscle tone. Fatigue-producing chemicals are cleared away and the nerve endings of the skin are soothed and relaxed.

The Joy of Massage

BASIC MASSAGE MOVES

Variation in movements is important for a top quality massage. The main moves you will use are:

Effleurage: Gliding the hands with long, even strokes over the surface of the skin. Generally a light, stimulating movement.

Tapotement: Short quick blows with your hands or fingers. These movements stimulate nerves and muscles, and boost circulation. Some of the techniques are:

> hacking – edge of palm
> slapping – flat of the hand
> tapping – fingertips
> cupping – cup-shaped hands
> beating – edge of fist

Petrissage: Kneading of muscle tissue. Includes pressing, squeezing, rolling and picking up muscles. Performed with hands and thumbs, and for small areas with thumb and forefinger.

Friction: Rapid, circular pressure over a particular area, using the palms or thumbs and fingertips.

Vibration: Rapid back and forth trembling pressure movements using either the fingers or hands.

❖

MASSAGE OIL

A good massage oil is light in texture and easily lubricates the skin to make stroking and kneading movements smooth and comfortable. This oil will moisturise the skin, relax and soothe tight muscles and ease muscular aches and pains.

Makes 500 mL (16 fl oz)

- ☐ **600 mL (1 pt) soya oil**
- ☐ **90 g (3 oz) fresh St John's Wort (leaves, stems and flowers)**
- ☐ **60 g (2 oz) fresh rose petals**

Pour oil into a large, wide-mouthed jar and add as many herbs and flowers, torn and chopped, as it will take. Seal and leave in a warm place for at least 2 days. Strain, squeeze out the herbs and discard, then repeat the procedure 10 more times. Store in a sealed glass bottle in a dark, cool place.

ALTERNATIVES

When making Massage Oil for face, neck and temples replace rose petals with lavender buds and leaves. If St John's Wort is difficult to obtain, substitute fresh oregano.

TO MASSAGE THE FEET

1 Place your hands side-by-side over ankle and perpendicular to it. Stroke down from ankle to toes, one hand after the other. Next, support foot with your knee underneath and place your hands on each ankle, thumbs resting on top. Commence circular kneading movements all around ankle and foot, then knead up and down the top part of foot with your thumbs, pressing sole from beneath with your fingers.

2 Move to toes and knead each one up and down between your thumb and forefinger. Then wrap your hands around foot, so your thumbs meet the sole while your fingers rest on the back, and knead entire sole between your thumbs and fingers. You will need to use good firm pressure, as the sole is a heavily padded spot.

3 Repeat procedure with other foot.

4 Have your partner turn face down and thumb-knead both soles.

5 Next, bring your thumbs up over the arch to Achilles tendon, kneading it in a circular motion from the heel up to calf. The final movement is knuckle-kneading: rest the flexed leg over your knees, hold foot in one hand, and knead sole and arch with the flat part of the knuckles of your other hand.

Apply good, strong pressure, digging in firmly, and working your way up and down in circles.

6   Repeat with other foot.

❖

MASSAGE SOAP

A soft massage soap that lubricates the skin for smooth and comfortable stroking and kneading.

Makes 250 g (8 oz)

- ☐ **250 g (8 oz) grated, pure coconut oil soap**
- ☐ **7 g (¼ oz) anhydrous lanolin**
- ☐ **1 teaspoon soya oil**
- ☐ **fragrant oil**

Place soap in the top of a double saucepan with just enough water to cover. Melt over a medium heat, stir thoroughly, then add lanolin and oil. Continue to stir until the lanolin has melted and all ingredients are well blended. Add a few drops of fragrant oil for scent and remove from heat. Pour liquid soap into large, wide-mouthed containers and allow to cool.

TO MASSAGE THE HEAD, NECK AND SHOULDERS

1   First focus on the neck: place your hands on one side of neck and make small circular movements with your fingers. Massage along sides and back of neck, from base of skull to shoulders. Repeat movements on other side of neck.

2   Cradle base of skull in both your hands, letting your thumbs hang free. Stroke back and forth on neck, pressing up against muscles. Without changing this position, begin to massage base of skull with your fingers using a vibrating motion.

3   Next place one hand over the top of your partner's head and the other at base of skull to support it. Press down with your top hand, moving it back and forth in circles. Go from hairline to back of head, then gently lift head and continue down back of neck. Finish massaging head by kneading scalp in small circular movements with your fingers. (Do not use oil on the scalp as it is self-lubricating.)

4   Place your fingertips over the top of shoulders, with your thumbs sitting on base of neck. Begin working your fingertips and thumbs well into muscles, then move over neck with your thumbs, using a rhythmic, circular, kneading movement. Work well into all tense areas on side of neck.

TO MASSAGE THE FACE

1   Start by placing one hand flat across your partner's forehead, fingers facing to the side. Stroke straight down to bridge of nose, simultaneously replacing the first hand with your other hand, giving a smooth, hand-over-hand action.

2   Next, place fingers of both hands on forehead, facing down toward eyes. Commence slow, circular, gentle kneading from middle of forehead to temples and sides of head.

3   Move to cheeks, place one hand on each of them, and gently massage with an oscillating movement, continuing down below jaw and chin area. Change to mouth and massage muscles firmly, yet gently, by circling lips with your index fingertips. Still using your fingertips, massage areas of the face you haven't yet reached.

4   Finish off by pressing all around the outer ear using the pads of the first two fingers. Continue the same movement under ear, with a bit more pressure on bony parts. Do this several times, then repeat on other ear.

10 WAYS TO MORE ENJOYABLE MASSAGE

1   Focus fully on the massage and on the person being massaged.

2   Support the body-part being massaged.

3   Try to keep all distractions and interruptions to an absolute minimum.

4   Ask your partner if there are any particular tension spots that need special attention.

5   Maintain a constant, even rhythm in your movements.

6   Silence is the golden rule – discussion about what you are doing will only interfere with full sensual appreciation.

7   Always remember to balance your movements.

8   When receiving a massage, empty your mind of all thoughts. Allow your body to hang loose, limp and relaxed.

9   For neck and shoulders, have a warm shower first.

10 Keep your partner warm. When you have finished massaging an area, cover with warm towels.

Everyone of us needs regular, restful, natural sleep to allow the body to unwind and restore energy. It is essential for good health and is a great complexion enhancer.

Sweet Dreams

WHY CAN'T YOU SLEEP?

Do you tend to overwork every day?

Do you feel almost too exhausted to get ready for bed?

You are creating a vicious circle of overtiredness, causing more fatigue the next day, which leads to an inability to relax and regenerate at night. Re-examine your daytime activities and establish a natural rhythm that allows your body to relax.

Is your bed comfortable?

Does your bed sag in the middle?

Is your mattress rock-hard?

Are your bedclothes too heavy?

All these are contributing factors in preventing you from having a restful night's sleep. Choose a bed that is comfortable, yet firm, and will provide adequate support for your spine. And in winter a feather duvet is warm and light.

Do you get sufficient fresh air at night?

Stuffy, dry rooms will leave you feeling jaded in the morning, dehydrate the skin, and can cause an accumulation of fluid around the eyes making them baggy when you awake.

Is your diet adequate?

Are you getting sufficient vitamins and minerals to soothe jangled nerves and tone up the nervous system?

Check your calcium and magnesium intake. Herbs can be included in your evening bath or taken as a tea to help promote sleep. Other herbs placed in a small sachet and slipped inside your pillow case have a calming effect.

In the bath: Bay leaf, chamomile, hyssop, lemon balm, lime flowers, lovage, pennyroyal, rosemary, valerian, yarrow.

As a tisane (tea): Aniseed, chamomile, elder flower, hops, lavender, red clover.

Made into a sleep pillow: Bay leaf, catmint, chamomile, clover, hops, lavender, lemon balm, lemon thyme, lemon verbena, marjoram, peppermint, sage.

IKEA

Tea Set Martinvale Fabric Signature

Herbal Teas

1 Combine red clover flower, dandelion and peppermint leaf. Place in a screwtop jar and store in a cool, dark cupboard.
2 To make tea, place 1 level teaspoon of the dried herb mixture for each person into a teapot, plus 1 for the pot, and pour in boiling water. Steep for 5 minutes, then strain into individual cups.

❖

HERBAL TEA

- ☐ **1 tablespoon fresh herbs or 1 teaspoon dried herbs of your choice per serve**
- ☐ **250 mL (8 fl oz) boiling water per serve**

1 For individual cups, place herbs in cup and pour in hot water, cover, infuse for 3 minutes, and strain into another cup.
2 When brewing in a teapot allow 1 serve per person and 1 for the pot. Infuse for 5 minutes in boiling water, then strain into individual cups.

Left: Choose a bed that is comfortable, yet firm and ensure that you get sufficient fresh air at night
Above: Herbal teas, if drunk regularly, will help you to feel and look good

❖

FLOWER TEA

- ☐ **250 mL (8 fl oz) boiling water per serve**
- ☐ **fresh flower petals**

Place water in a saucepan and bring to the boil. Add flower petals, replace lid, and simmer for 1 minute. Remove from heat and allow to steep for 3 minutes, then strain into individual cups.

❖

TEA REPLACER

- ☐ **4 tablespoons dried red clover flower**
- ☐ **4 tablespoons dried dandelion leaf**
- ☐ **4 tablespoons dried peppermint leaf**

❖

DANDELION COFFEE

Dandelion makes an excellent herbal substitute for coffee that not only provides a healthy alternative, but will also act as a general tonic.

Oven temperature 200°C, 400° F, Gas 6

- ☐ **dandelion roots, washed and dried**

1 Cut dandelion roots into rings about 2 cm thick. Place pieces in a roasting dish and roast for 20 minutes.
2 Remove from oven and set aside to cool then place in a coffee bean grinder, food processor or blender and process to reduce to granules. Use in the same way as instant coffee.

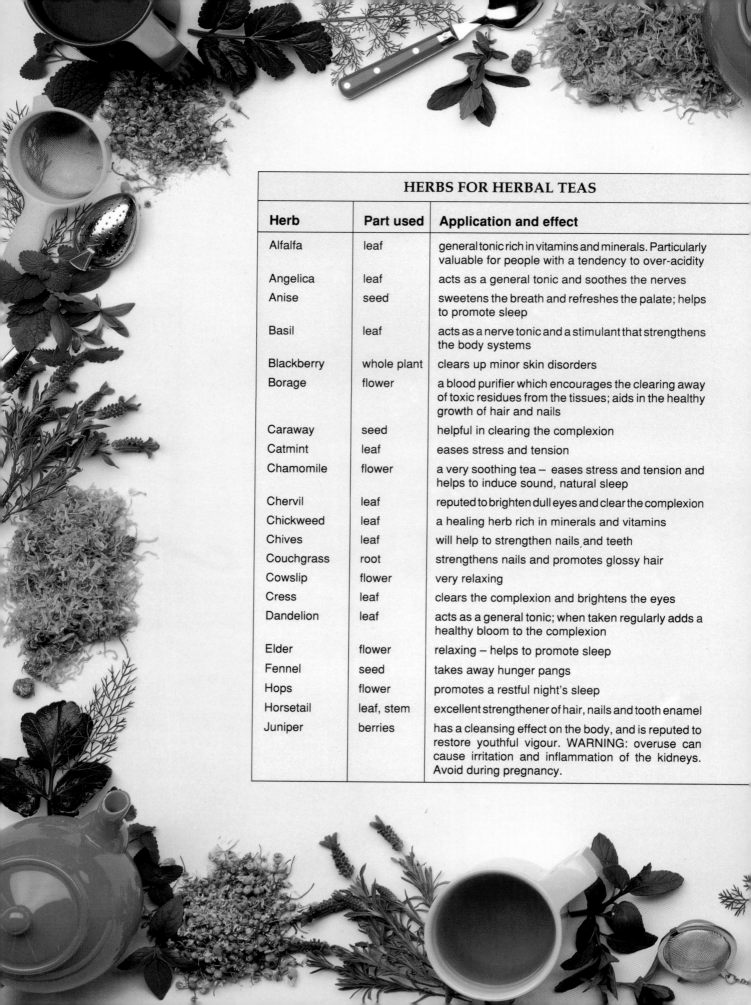

HERBS FOR HERBAL TEAS

Herb	Part used	Application and effect
Alfalfa	leaf	general tonic rich in vitamins and minerals. Particularly valuable for people with a tendency to over-acidity
Angelica	leaf	acts as a general tonic and soothes the nerves
Anise	seed	sweetens the breath and refreshes the palate; helps to promote sleep
Basil	leaf	acts as a nerve tonic and a stimulant that strengthens the body systems
Blackberry	whole plant	clears up minor skin disorders
Borage	flower	a blood purifier which encourages the clearing away of toxic residues from the tissues; aids in the healthy growth of hair and nails
Caraway	seed	helpful in clearing the complexion
Catmint	leaf	eases stress and tension
Chamomile	flower	a very soothing tea – eases stress and tension and helps to induce sound, natural sleep
Chervil	leaf	reputed to brighten dull eyes and clear the complexion
Chickweed	leaf	a healing herb rich in minerals and vitamins
Chives	leaf	will help to strengthen nails and teeth
Couchgrass	root	strengthens nails and promotes glossy hair
Cowslip	flower	very relaxing
Cress	leaf	clears the complexion and brightens the eyes
Dandelion	leaf	acts as a general tonic; when taken regularly adds a healthy bloom to the complexion
Elder	flower	relaxing – helps to promote sleep
Fennel	seed	takes away hunger pangs
Hops	flower	promotes a restful night's sleep
Horsetail	leaf, stem	excellent strengthener of hair, nails and tooth enamel
Juniper	berries	has a cleansing effect on the body, and is reputed to restore youthful vigour. WARNING: overuse can cause irritation and inflammation of the kidneys. Avoid during pregnancy.

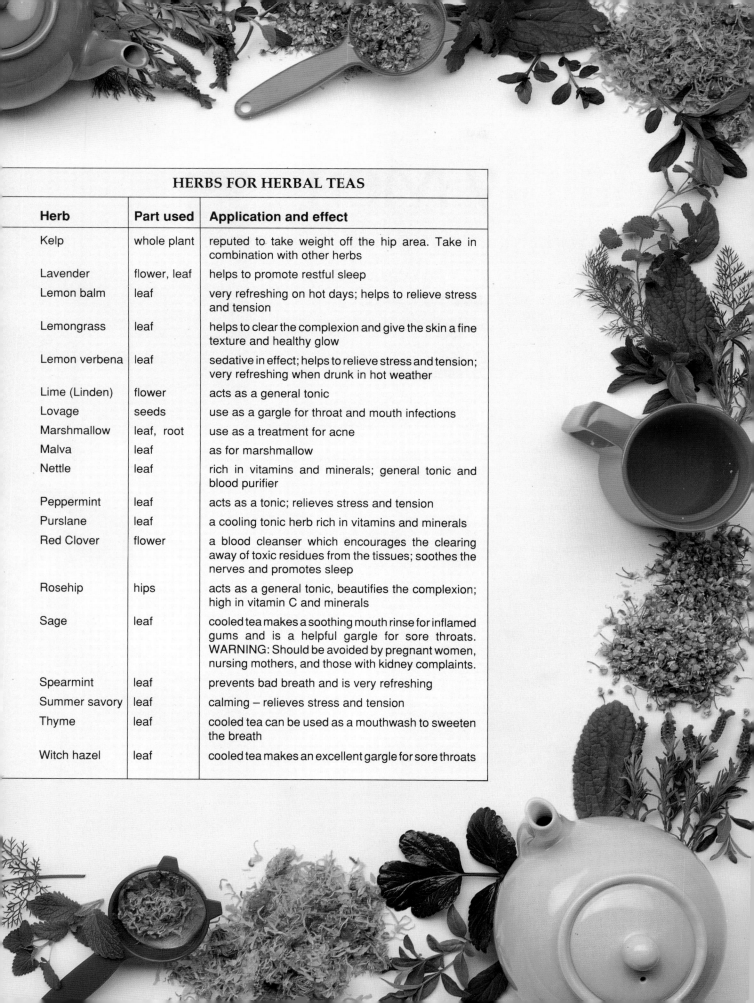

HERBS FOR HERBAL TEAS

Herb	Part used	Application and effect
Kelp	whole plant	reputed to take weight off the hip area. Take in combination with other herbs
Lavender	flower, leaf	helps to promote restful sleep
Lemon balm	leaf	very refreshing on hot days; helps to relieve stress and tension
Lemongrass	leaf	helps to clear the complexion and give the skin a fine texture and healthy glow
Lemon verbena	leaf	sedative in effect; helps to relieve stress and tension; very refreshing when drunk in hot weather
Lime (Linden)	flower	acts as a general tonic
Lovage	seeds	use as a gargle for throat and mouth infections
Marshmallow	leaf, root	use as a treatment for acne
Malva	leaf	as for marshmallow
Nettle	leaf	rich in vitamins and minerals; general tonic and blood purifier
Peppermint	leaf	acts as a tonic; relieves stress and tension
Purslane	leaf	a cooling tonic herb rich in vitamins and minerals
Red Clover	flower	a blood cleanser which encourages the clearing away of toxic residues from the tissues; soothes the nerves and promotes sleep
Rosehip	hips	acts as a general tonic, beautifies the complexion; high in vitamin C and minerals
Sage	leaf	cooled tea makes a soothing mouth rinse for inflamed gums and is a helpful gargle for sore throats. WARNING: Should be avoided by pregnant women, nursing mothers, and those with kidney complaints.
Spearmint	leaf	prevents bad breath and is very refreshing
Summer savory	leaf	calming – relieves stress and tension
Thyme	leaf	cooled tea can be used as a mouthwash to sweeten the breath
Witch hazel	leaf	cooled tea makes an excellent gargle for sore throats

Today's man is starting to take care of his skin, hair, hands and nails. While all the recipes in this book may be used by men and women, these recipes have been specially formulated with men in mind.

Mainly Men

❖
PRE-SHAVE MOISTURISER

A pre-shave moisturiser replaces oils lost from the skin through cleansing and will aid in the prevention of razor-drag and skin damage.

Makes 125 mL (4 fl oz)

- [ ] **15 g ($^1/_2$ oz) beeswax**
- [ ] **3 tablespoons almond oil**
- [ ] **1$^1/_2$ tablespoons wheat germ oil**
- [ ] **2 tablespoons rosewater**
- [ ] **1 teaspoon lemon juice**

1   Melt wax, almond and wheat germ oils in the top of a double boiler over a low heat. When completely liquid stir in rosewater and lemon juice and stir until well blended.
2   Remove from heat and beat continually until cool. Store in a sterilised, screwtop jar.
3   To use, massage well into face and neck 10 minutes before shaving.

❖
SHAVING SOAP

Makes 1 cake

- [ ] **100 g (3$^1/_2$ oz) grated pure white soap**
- [ ] **distilled water**
- [ ] **4 drops of essential oil of lavender**
- [ ] **2 drops of essential oil of thyme**
- [ ] **1 drop of essential oil of peppermint**
- [ ] **5 drops of essential oil of bergamot**

Melt soap in an enamel pan, over a low heat with just enough water to form a soft paste (use a potato masher to help dissolve soap). Stir in essential oils, until well blended, remove from heat and spoon into a wide-mouthed, shallow container. Allow soap to harden for 48 hours before use.

❖
SHAVING CREAM

Makes 500 mL (16 fl oz)

- [ ] **4 tablespoons grated pure white soap**
- [ ] **water**
- [ ] **170 mL (5$^1/_2$ oz) rosewater**
- [ ] **170 mL (5$^1/_2$ oz) vodka**

Melt soap in an enamel pan, over a low heat with just enough water to form a soft paste when cold. Dissolve rosewater in alcohol and mix with soap paste. Store in a wide-mouthed, screwtop jar.

SUN CARE
The sun is one of the most damaging elements. If overexposed to the sun our skin becomes dry and wrinkled, and the risk of skin cancer increases. Remember, when in the sun always:
✧ Wear a wide-brimmed hat;
✧ Apply a good sunscreen;
✧ Wear a shirt to prevent sunburn.

Today's man is taking much greater care of his skin. Make these natural products for the man in your life.

Shaving Coat, Shaving Set and Soap Dish Made Where Towel Powder Blue Bottles Martinvale Small Jar Villeroy & Boch

It is worth spending a little time making pretty packages for your beautiful homemade comestics, especially if you are giving them as a gift. Choose colours that will match your bedroom or bathroom.

Pretty Packaging

PRESENTATION BASKET

To really present these fragrant and delightful mixtures prettily, package them in a wicker basket, perhaps lined with straw, shredded paper or tissue. Add ribbons and wrap the whole basket with cellophane and tie another bow to hold the wrapping. Make this basket look masculine or feminine by the choice of ribbons and basket.

❖

ACID ETCHING

This method of decoration is only suitable for treating glass containers.

MATERIALS

☐ **acid etching paste (available from most stained-glass specialist shops)**
☐ **stick-on stencils**
☐ **small paintbrush**

METHOD

Apply the stick-on stencil in the desired position, wear rubber gloves and coat the design with acid etching paste. Allow paste to dry overnight, then wash off under running warm water. Peel off stencil, dry jar or bottle, then decorate with swing tag and ribbon bow if desired.

To make your own stick-on stencil: using commercially available adhesive-backed vinyl paper with a peel-off backing sheet, draw stencil design on backing sheet, then cut away design area using a sharp craft knife. Peel off backing paper and apply stick-on paper stencil to glass. Proceed to etch as above.

Ribbons Offray Fabrics Liberty

❖ DECOUPAGE

Suitable for application to plastic, glass, wood, heavy paper and pottery.

MATERIALS
- [ ] **decorative paper with simple motifs**
- [ ] **PVA adhesive (polyvinyl acetate adhesive)**
- [ ] **small paintbrush**
- [ ] **small sharp scissors**
- [ ] **clear spray paint (optional)**

METHOD
Cut out motifs from greeting cards, wrapping paper or similar, either being very precise, or leaving a small margin around the outside of the motif. Using PVA adhesive, coat back of motif then position it. Coat the motif with adhesive. (This glue is white and milky in substance, but dries clear and shiny.) Either coat the whole bottle or jar with glue and allow to dry, or spray with clear paint. Add ribbons and swing tags, or decorate a label with more motifs then apply to bottle or jar.

❖ PAINTING

Most surfaces can be painted, though containers that come in contact with moisture need specific paints.

MATERIALS
- [ ] **water-resistant paints that are specifically suitable for application to glass, plastic or metal, (these are usually sold at artists' supply shops, or you may use paints that are applied to children's models; they are resilient paints usually packaged in small quantities)**
- [ ] **small paintbrushes**
- [ ] **chinagraph pencil for outlining design**

METHOD
Draw design onto container using pencil, then paint with desired colours.

LABELS AND SWING TAGS
All containers need a label, to define their contents and purpose. They can be pre-decorated purchased labels, or ones that you have cut out and decorated yourself. Make them from used greeting cards or any other firm cardboard. For a swing tag, make a hole at the top corner closest to the bottle or jar, using a hole punch, then thread ribbon through and tie around the neck of the bottle. Make stick-on labels in interesting shapes, say a flower or geometric shape, then glue to container.

OTHER IDEAS
Apply the following materials to containers and labels. Use PVA adhesive or a glue gun where appropriate.
- ✧ Dried or pressed flowers glued to containers or labels.
- ✧ Strips of ribbon or lace tied around the neck of bottles or jars.
- ✧ Ribbons tied into bows on the lids.
- ✧ Simple stick-on stars and dots all over containers.

Attractive packaging adds the final touch to your beautiful homemade cosmetics

Herbal Dictionary

Aloe vera (*Aloe barbadensis*)
Its unique healing qualities keep the skin fresh and young, soften ageing lines, and is said to be an excellent hair conditioner.

Basil (*Ocimum basilicum*)
Makes a refreshing tea which clears the head and acts as a general stimulant. Combined with borage it helps to relieve stress and tension.

Bergamot (*Monarda didyma*)
The leaves make a refreshing and fragrant addition to bath water, and when made into a tisane (tea) with milk is reputed to induce sleep.

Borage (*Borago officinalis*)
As a facial steam it improves dry, sensitive skin, and when taken as a tea promotes the growth of healthy hair and nails.

Chamomile (*Matricaria chamomilla*)
As a tea it is very soothing, easing tension and promoting sound natural sleep. Added to bath water it will relieve sunburn, leave the skin smooth and soft, and soothe tired and aching muscles. And as a hair rinse, it will lighten and condition blonde hair.

Chickweed (*Stellaria media*)
Applied externally it is a remedy for sores, skin irritations and eczema, and can be used in acne preparations.

Comfrey (*Symphytum officinale*)
The leaves or roots are used in herbal cosmetics to remove wrinkles and rejuvenate ageing skin.

Dandelion (*Taraxacum officinale*)
Taken regularly as a tea it will add a healthy bloom to your complexion.

Elder (*Sambucus nigra*)
Elder flower water is used externally as an eyewash, a bath additive and a skin toner. It can be used in herbal cosmetics, will help to smooth roughened skin, soothe sunburn, clear up minor skin infections, and is reputed to remove wrinkles.

Fennel (*Foeniculum vulgare*)
An infusion of the seeds makes a soothing eyewash, and can be used as a general skin freshener and wrinkle remover.

Lady's mantle (*Alchemilla vulgaris*)
The herb is an astringent and the freshly pressed juice is helpful in the treatment of acne.

Lavender (*Lavandula officinalis*)
It is stimulating and antiseptic, and can be used as a skin tonic for oily skin. Lavender oil is good for the hair.

Lemon balm (*Melissa officinalis*)
A cleansing and antiseptic herb for the face, the hair or in the bath.

Lemongrass (*Cymbopogon citratus*)
Can be used in herbal cosmetics to normalise the sebaceous glands.

Lemon verbena (*Lippia citriodora*)
An astringent herb for the hair and the skin around the eyes.

Lovage (*Levisticum officinale*)
Has a deodorant effect on the skin when added to the bath or applied under the arms.

Marigold (*Calendula officinalis*)
Remarkably healing to the skin as an oil or when included in herbal cosmetics.

Nettle (*Urtica dioica*)
A skin and hair tonic and stimulant, nettle encourages circulation.

Parsley (*Petroselinum crispum*)
Cleansing and soothing, and beneficial to the face, the eyes, the hair, and as a deodorant.

Rose (*Rosa species*)
Rosewater hydrates the skin and is cleansing and mildly astringent.

Rosemary (*Rosmarinus officinalis*)
Cleansing and stimulating, and beneficial to hair. Also a deodorant, mouthwash, and bath herb.

Sage (*Salvia officinalis*)
It is a deodorant, strengthens the gums, and polishes and whitens teeth.

St John's Wort (*Hypericum perforatum*)
Valued mainly for its oil, which is soothing and healing.

Southernwood (*Artemisia abrotanum*)
Combined with rosemary it is a good tonic to encourage hair growth.

Spearmint (*Mentha spicata*)
An infusion makes a good skin lotion to improve the complexion and soothe roughened skin.

Thyme (*Thymus vulgaris*)
Can be occasionally used as a facial tonic, as it encourages the flow of blood to the surface of the skin.

Witch hazel (*Hamamelis virginiana*)
Can be made into an astringent lotion that will help reduce the size of large pores. Useful as an underarm deodorant.

Yarrow (*Achillea millefolium*)
Makes a very good cleanser for greasy skin and pimples. It can also be used for chapped hands and sore nipples.

Essentials

HERBAL SUPPLIERS

This list of suppliers is not intended to be comprehensive. It is a guide to enable you to locate the ingredients you will need. The Yellow Pages for your area will reveal further contacts.

G. Baldwin and Co
171/173 Walworth Road London SE17 1RW
Tel: (071) 703 5550

Neal's Yard Apothecary
2 Neal's Yard, Covent Garden,
London WC2 9DP
Tel: (071) 379 7222

D. Napier and Sons Ltd
17/18 Bristo Place, Edinburgh,
Scotland EHI 2QZ
Tel: (031) 225 5542

Self-Heal Herbs
Hayes Corner, South Cheriton,
Templecombe, Somerset 8A8 OBR
Tel: (0963) 70300

HOMEOPATHIC PHARMACIES

Ainsworths
38 New Cavendish Street, London W1M 7LH
Tel: (071) 935 5330

Helios Homeopathic Pharmacy
92 Camden Road, Tunbridge Wells,
Kent TN1 2AP
Tel: (0892) 36393

A. Nelson and Co Ltd
5 Endeavor Way, Wimbledon,
London SW19 9UH
Tel: (081) 946 8527

Weleda (UK) Ltd
Heanor Road, Ilkeston, Derbyshire DE7 8DR
Tel: (0602) 303 151

MEDICAL HERBALISM

The National Institute of Medical Herbalists,
34 Cambridge Road, London SW 11 4RR
Tel: (071) 228 4417

HEALTH FOOD STORES

Holland and Barrett
Canada Road, Byfleet, Surrey KT14 7JL
Tel: 0932 336 022

MISCELLANEOUS

Health food shop: vegetable and seed oils; herbal oils; oatmeal; aloe vera juice; cider and white wine vinegar; almond meal; brewer's yeast
Pharmacy: anhydrous lanolin; magnesium carbonate; French chalk; liquid coconut oil; elder flower water; glycerine; calcium carbonate; gum tragacanth; fuller's earth; rosewater; witch hazel solution
Herb nurseries: orris root powder; fresh herbs; herb plants; dried herbs; herbal oils

MEASURING DRY INGREDIENTS

Metric	Imperial
15 g	$1/2$ oz
30 g	1 oz
60 g	2 oz
90 g	3 oz
125 g	4 oz
155 g	5 oz
185 g	6 oz
220 g	7 oz
250 g	8 oz
280 g	9 oz
315 g	10 oz
375 g	12 oz
410 g	13 oz
440 g	14 oz
470 g	15 oz
500 g	16 oz (1 lb)
750 g	1 lb 8 oz
1 kg	2 lb
1.5 kg	3 lb

METRIC CUPS & SPOONS

Metric	Cups	Imperial
60 mL	$1/4$ cup	2 fl oz
80 mL	$1/3$ cup	$2 1/2$ fl oz
125 mL	$1/2$ cup	4 fl oz
250 mL	1 cup	8 fl oz
	Spoons	
1.25 mL	$1/4$ teaspoon	
2.5 mL	$1/2$ teaspoon	
5 mL	1 teaspoon	
20 mL	1 tablespoon	

QUICK CONVERTER

Metric	Imperial
5 mm	$1/4$ in
1 cm	$1/2$ in
2 cm	$3/4$ in
2.5 cm	1 in
5 cm	2 in
10 cm	4 in
15 cm	6 in
20 cm	8 in
23 cm	9 in
25 cm	10 in
30 cm	12 in

OVEN TEMPERATURES

°C	°F	Gas Mark
120	250	$1/2$
140	275	1
150	300	2
160	325	3
180	350	4
190	375	5
200	400	6
220	425	7
240	475	8
250	500	9

MEASURING LIQUIDS

Metric	Imperial	Cup
30 mL	1 fl oz	
60 mL	2 fl oz	$1/4$ cup
90 mL	3 fl oz	
125 mL	4 fl oz	$1/2$ cup
155 mL	5 fl oz	
170 mL	$5 1/2$ fl oz	$2/3$ cup
185 mL	6 fl oz	
220 mL	7 fl oz	
250 mL	8 fl oz	1 cup
500 mL	16 fl oz	2 cups
600 mL	20 fl oz (1 pt)	
750 mL	$1 1/4$ pt	
1 litre	$1 3/4$ pt	4 cups
1.2 litres	2 pt	

Index

ACKNOWLEDGEMENTS
The publishers wish to thank the following Admiral Appliances; Black & Decker (Australasia) Pty Ltd; Blanco Appliances; Knebel Kitchens; Leigh Mardon Pty Ltd; Master Foods of Australia; Meadow Lea Foods; Namco Cookware; Ricegrowers' Co-op Mills Ltd; Sunbeam Corporation Ltd; Tycraft Pty Ltd distributors of Braun, Australia; White Wings Foods for their assistance during recipe testing.

Penny Cox for her assistance during recipe testing.

COVER
Ashley Mackevicius (photography), Wendy Berecry (Styling). Plate from Villeroy and Boch, Towel, Hair Combs and Soap from Linen and Lace